The macroeconomy
A guide for business

KEITH CUTHBERTSON and
PETER GRIPAIOS

2nd Edition

London and New York

First published 1988 by HarperCollins Academic

Second edition first published 1993
by Routledge
11 New Fetter Lane, London EC4P 4EE

Simultaneously published in the USA and Canada
by Routledge
a division of Routledge, Chapman and Hall Inc.
29 West 35th Street, New York, NY 10001

© 1988, 1993 Keith Cuthbertson and Peter Gripaios

Typeset by Witwell Ltd, Southport
Printed and bound in Great Britain by
Biddles Ltd, Guildford and King's Lynn

British Library Cataloguing in Publication Data

A catalogue reference for this book is available from the British Library

ISBN 0–415–08672–8Hb
      0–415–08673–6Pb

*Library of Congress Cataloging in Publication Data
has been applied for.*

ISBN 0–415–08672–8Hb
      0–415–08673–6Pb

Contents

Figures

Tables

Glossary

C	=	consumer's expenditure (real)
DC	=	direct cost
dc	=	ln (DC)
F	=	forward exchange rate
f	=	ln (F)
Ln	=	natural logarithm
M	=	money supply
Δm	=	rate of money supply growth
P	=	aggregate price level (domestic)
P*	=	aggregate price level (foreign)
p	=	ln (P)
Δp	=	rate of inflation
R	=	simple correlation coefficient (Chapter 5 only)
R	=	yield to maturity on a bond
r	=	interest rate (domestic)
r*	=	interest rate (foreign)
S	=	spot exchange rate
s	=	ln (S)
$\bar{s}$	=	long-run level of exchange rate in logarithms
Δs	=	percentage change in the exchange rate
U	=	actual unemployment (%)
U_0	=	natural rate of unemployment or NAIRU
W	=	level of nominal wages
WL	=	nominal wealth
Δw	=	rate of wage inflation
x_p	=	rate of productivity growth (total)
x_w	=	rate of growth in labour productivity
Y	=	level of real output (GDP) or income
Y_0	=	natural rate of output
θ	=	risk premium

μ =   expected appreciation of the home currency ($\equiv s_{t+1}^{e} - s_t$)

Superscript 'e' indicates expected value of a variable (for example, Δp^{e} = expected rate of inflation)

1 Introduction

There are, of course, numerous economics texts designed for the economics specialist but to our knowledge few designed specifically for businessmen or students in the business area. And yet economics has very often been an important component of degrees in subjects such as business studies, accountancy and marketing, and of professional courses. In our opinion, there is a huge gap between the economics taught on a specialist economics degree course and the economic concepts that are used by businessmen and even business economists. Frequently, the complaint of business-orientated students is the lack of relevance of much of the economics taught in conventional courses. However, the subject-matter of economics and, in our opinion, macroeconomics in particular is of crucial importance to the practising businessman. The challenge is, therefore, to design a useful course in macroeconomics for business, bearing in mind both the non-specialist audience and the typically limited time to get the message across. We have, therefore, attempted to produce a book that does this.

The book is developed as follows. We begin by laying down some theoretical foundations, which will be useful for understanding the applied chapters that constitute the rest of the book. The latter begin with an examination of macroeconomic risk including the business cycle and its effects on business. It is suggested that the macroeconomic environment is of great importance to business profitability and it is, therefore, crucial that the businessman understands that environment.

Of particular importance is strategic planning by business and this brings us on to the role of forecasting. We therefore examine the role of macroeconomic forecasts in business decisions and why and how forecasts differ. The chapter concludes with a description of methods of assessing the sensitivity of forecasts to different assumptions and points out that the individual businessman is now able to undertake such an analysis on personal computers. We then turn to a detailed examination of the international environment with two chapters on the exchange rate. The first of these is primarily concerned with how a firm should cope with 'exchange risk' while the second mainly focuses on interpreting and understanding movements in the exchange rate.

The next chapter deals with the financial environment and examines in turn microeconomic aspects of financial decision-taking, the financial institutions and the determination of interest rates. We then move on to the determination of price and wage inflation with an examination of both theoretical and empirical models.

Policy considerations are given detailed consideration after this. One chapter focuses on the impact of fiscal and monetary policy and highlights the transmission mechanism whereby government policy influences the overall level of prices, wages, interest rates, output and other key macroeconomic variables. Specific examples of real-world model simulations are given, but more importantly the reader is encouraged to cast a critical eye over any forecast that may be presented to him as part of an underlying business strategy. We then discuss the implications for the conduct of macroeconomy policy of the UK entry into the exchange rate mechanism (ERM), and the possible adoption of a single European currency ('the Gazza'). The second policy chapter is concerned with controversies regarding the role of economic policy in economic growth, which is of clear importance to businessmen. The overview then brings together the points made in previous chapters in the context of improving knowledge and control of the business environment.

Where possible the intention has been to make the book free standing, although readers would certainly benefit from having studied an introductory book on economics and possibly also one on introductory statistics.

The new edition differs in a number of respects from the first. The theoretical section that formerly comprised part of the chapter on 'use of forecasts' now becomes a chapter in its own right. Some of the material of the original Chapter 2 now appears in other parts of the book. The chapter on the financial environment now contains a discussion of volatility in the stock and foreign-exchange markets and the possible influence of 'fads' or bubbles in causing excessive price movements. We have included a substantial new section on the European Monetary System in Chapter 9. Another feature of the new edition is the inclusion of self-assessment questions. Some of these require an extension of the material outlined in the text and can be used in conjunction with the further reading referred to, as well as other sources such as recent journal and newspaper articles.

We hope that the book will, at the very least, enable businessmen and business students to understand economic articles in the press. They may even be able to answer the questions of the man in the pub satisfactorily, something far too few economics graduates are able to do.

2 Economic foundations

Many people think of economics as an exact science and find it extremely irritating that one group of economists disagrees with another group and that economists and, therefore, the governments that they advise so often get things wrong. The fact is, however, that the nature of economic relationships is extremely complex and, therefore, difficult to fathom. Moreover, what may be true at one period is not necessarily true at others, for behaviour is sometimes altered quite dramatically in response to changes in fashion, tastes and other economic shocks.

This all gives plenty of scope for individual economists to hold different theoretical perceptions regarding which economic variables are most important, which economic variable is affected by which other economic variable(s) and to what extent and for what reason at a particular time. It has also made such perceptions difficult to refute by statistical testing despite early optimism that such refutation would be possible. In short, economics, despite a sizeable scientific component, remains very much an art and we should not expect it to be otherwise.

Nevertheless, the effects of the art are obvious in the form of economic forecasts and economic policies, and the latter, in particular, can affect the livelihood of millions. It is of some importance, therefore, that some time is spent looking at the important schools of economic thought. To do this we utilize the simple tools of aggregate demand and supply.

2.1 THEORETICAL FOUNDATIONS

Aggregate demand

Aggregate demand is defined as the sum of consumption, investment, government expenditure and exports less imports of goods. The aggregate demand (AD) function relates total demand in the economy to the variables that affect it. The AD curve relates AD to one of these, i.e. the price level, which is defined as the average price of all the goods produced in the economy. The curve is assumed to be downward sloping, as depicted in Figure 2.1, for the following reasons.

The so-called 'Pigou' effect (real (money) balance effect)

A fall in the price level increases the real value of money balances. As the purchasing power of money has increased, this leads to an increase in consumers' expenditure. As consumption is a component of aggregate demand, aggregate demand rises. This also applies to financial assets other than money (e.g. bonds, building society deposits). It is then termed a wealth effect.

The real income effect

A fall in prices increases the purchasing power of those on fixed incomes who are, therefore, encouraged to spend more.

The export effect

A fall in a country's prices, if unmatched by price changes in other countries or by an appreciation in the exchange rate, will improve the price competitiveness of the first country's goods and should increase export demand. However, this is likely to be a 'short-term' effect (albeit lasting some three to five years) since under floating exchange rates there is a tendency for the real exchange rate (competitiveness) to remain constant (see Chapter 5).

The interest rate effect

A fall in prices implies that people and firms need to hold smaller money balances for transactions reasons. They therefore buy bonds (e.g. via life assurance policies, which life assurance and pension funds then invest in bonds), bond prices rise and interest rates fall. The latter leads to more investment and consumption (see Chapter 7).

The aggregate demand curve will shift in response to changes in any of the non-price factors that affect the components of the AD function (e.g. consumption). Other than the price level (which determines the slope), these include government expenditure, the nominal money supply, autonomous investment and changes in the level of world trade working via an increase in exports.

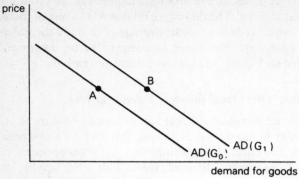

Figure 2.1 Aggregate demand

A rise in, say, government expenditure leads to a higher level of demand (at each price level) via the familiar multiplier process (A to B in Figure 2.1).

Aggregate supply

This depicts what firms would wish to supply given changes in the factors affecting supply. The relationship between aggregate supply and price is the subject of great controversy. The following views exist.

The AS curve is vertical

This is the so-called neo-classical case and is illustrated in Figure 2.2. Output is assumed to be at the full employment level, Y_f. In the neo-classical model, full employment is where labour demand equals labour supply at a market-clearing real wage as indicated in Figure 2.3. The upward-sloping labour supply curve indicates that as workers are offered an increased real wage (i.e. purchasing power over goods) they are willing to undertake more overtime, and other 'workers' (particularly married women and young people) are encouraged to leave the ranks of the unemployed. The labour supply curve will shift to the right as the population of working age increases and as welfare benefits fall relative to wages. The downward-sloping labour demand curve is a consequence of the assumption that firms maximize profits. The revenue earned by a worker is equal to his output (per year) multiplied by the price, P, of that output. As nominal wages, W, fall for a fixed price level – t iat is real wages, W/P, fall – the workers 'price themselves into jobs', earning more profit (per man) for the firm.

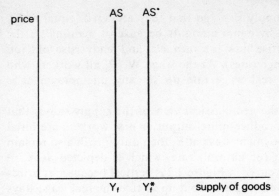

Figure 2.2 The vertical aggregate supply curve

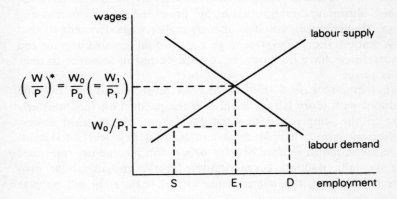

Figure 2.3 Labour demand and supply

Firms therefore increase their demand for labour: the labour demand schedule is downward sloping. The labour demand curve shifts to the right as the productivity of labour increases (e.g. as better capital equipment is installed).

In the neo-classical model there will be some unemployment at an employment level E_1. However, this is frictional or voluntary unemployment, as workers change jobs and search for better job offers. Employment tends to return to E_1 in this model because wages and prices are assumed to be perfectly flexible. Hence, if we are momentarily at a lower real wage, W_0/P_1, the demand for labour, D, exceeds the supply, S. Hence, firms bid for workers and raise their wage offers to W_1. As they do so the real wage rises back to W_1/P_1 ($=W_0/P_0$). Demand for labour falls and supply rises, so that they are again equal at E_1. Prices and wages rise by equal amounts because of 'bidding' in the market (i.e firms advertise 'new' job vacancies and readvertise 'old' job vacancies at higher wage rates). At the wage W_1/P_1 all workers who wish to work at this real wage rate do so: any unemployment is voluntary.

The final strand in the neo-classical view of the supply side is that firms simultaneously produce more output as new workers are hired and, therefore, if employment stays at E_1 then output will also remain at its full employment (or natural) rate, which is depicted as Y_f in Figure 2.2. The supply curve in Figure 2.2 is vertical because, as prices rise (as described above), wages are bid up so that the real wage stays at $(W/P)^*$ and employment and hence output remain at E_1 and Y_f respectively.

The latter scenario happens because workers do not suffer from 'money' illusion and realize that higher prices reduce their purchasing power. Higher prices would be met by higher wage demands so that profit margins (i.e. prices over wage costs) would remain constant and manufacturers have no incentive to raise output in response to their higher prices.

What might cause a shift in AS? As more output can only be produced with more labour input (i.e. the production function) any shifts in the supply and demand for labour curves yield a new equilibrium level of employment and hence a new level of output. Therefore, a fall in welfare benefits or a cut in income tax rates that shift the labour-supply curve rightwards or a rise in labour productivity that shifts the labour-demand curve to the right will increase the equilibrium (or 'natural') rate of employment and output.

This raises the natural rate of employment above E_1 in Figure 2.3 and so shifts AS (Figure 2.2) to AS*. Hence in the neo-classical model it is only these 'supply-side' policies that lead to changes in output. (Note that increasing the productivity of labour and hence shifting the labour demand curve outwards is classified as a 'supply-side' policy.)

The AS curve is horizontal

This is the extreme Keynesian case as shown in Figure 2.4 and may apply when there are many unemployed resources. Firms expand output even though prices remain unchanged and workers will be prepared to work more at the existing nominal wage. This is only likely to occur in a deep recession.

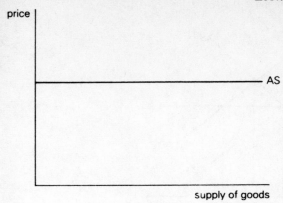

Figure 2.4 The horizontal aggregate supply curve

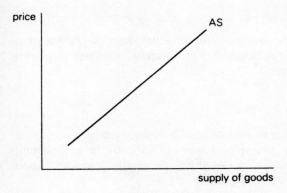

Figure 2.5 An upward-sloping aggregate supply curve

The upward-sloping curve

In this case (Figure 2.5), rising prices call forth increases in output. This situation would occur if the rising prices increased the perceived profitability of producing more goods (i.e. the profit margin over wage costs, P/W, increased or equivalently the real wage, W/P, fell). This would happen if selling prices rose more than production costs because:

1 workers were interested in money rather than real wages;
2 workers' expectations of the price level lagged behind its actual value;

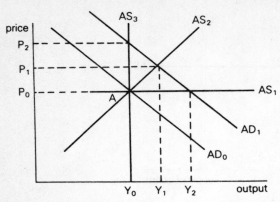

Figure 2.6 Equilibrium of aggregate demand and supply

3 institutional factors stopped wages increasing as fast as prices.

Clearly, if some of these factors are true in the short run rather than the long then we have the possibility of different long- and short-run aggregate supply curves.

The complete model

Figure 2.6 traces out the impact of a shift in aggregate demand from AD_0 to AD_1, say, for example, due to an increase in government spending. It demonstrates that the result is crucially dependent upon the assumed slope of the supply curve.

We start at point A with $P = P_0$ and $Y = Y_0$:

1 if $AS = AS_1$ we have a pure output effect from Y_0 to Y_2;
2 if $AS = AS_2$ we have an increase in both output to Y_1 and the price level to P_1; and
3 if $AS = AS_3$ we have a pure price effect from P_0 to P_2.

It is usually argued that the result of an increase in AD will differ in the long and short runs as suggested above and depicted in Figure 2.7.

Thus a shift in AD from AD_0 to AD_1 may result in an increase in output if workers fail to realize the extent to which prices are rising, or if they are temporarily 'locked' into wage agreements. They therefore supply more in response to rising or constant money wages (but falling real wages) and we move from point A to point B on the short-term supply curve, SAS_0. Workers cannot, however, be duped in the long

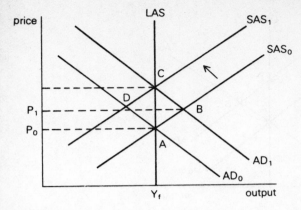

Figure 2.7 Long- and short-run equilibria

run and eventually they choose to supply less labour at the current (new) price level, P_1. The result is a shift in the short-run curve to SAS_1 and a movement to C. The long-run curve joins points of equilibrium such as A and C, although it may or may not be vertical as indicated above.

The main points of contention concern this issue and also the length of time involved in the long and short run. We now examine these issues further by using Figure 2.7 to explain some of the differences in monetarist, rational expectations and Keynesian thought. It should be emphasized that there are a great many shades of opinion and that, in practice, boundaries are blurred. Our aim, therefore, is to depict the essence of the different schools of thought.

2.2 SCHOOLS OF THOUGHT

Monetarist

The essence of the orthodox monetarist position is that any expansion of aggregate demand by, for example, an increase in the money supply (in excess of growth in real output) or an increase in government expenditure is likely to affect only prices in the long run. Thus, we would eventually move from point A to point C with output remaining at Y_f. This is regarded as the 'natural' rate of output and is determined by the productive potential of the economy. This, in turn, is determined by labour productivity and the position of the labour-demand curve in Figure 2.3. More capital equipment or improved managerial

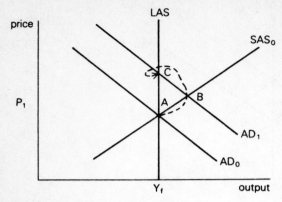

Figure 2.8 The monetarist view

and working practices can slowly increase labour productivity, move the demand for labour outwards and hence also move the LAS curve to the right.

Because the money supply only influences prices in the long run this is known as the neutrality proposition. The fact that government expenditure does not influence output in the long run is known as (complete) crowding out.

Orthodox monetarists recognize that there may, however, be short-run effects which mean that the process of adjustment from one long-run equilibrium (at A) to another (at C) may be complicated and unpredictable (Figure 2.8). They envisage a movement to B as firms and workers make mistakes in anticipating the (general) rise in prices. Firms, therefore, overestimate expected profits and wish to supply more goods and workers overestimate the purchasing power of their nominal wages and are willing to produce more. For example, suppose SAS_0 reflects what would be supplied given an expected price level of P_0. The actual prices rise to P_1 given the shift in AD and the movement from A to B. Expectations will now change given the new observed price level. In other words, workers learn from their past errors and in future periods they recognize that, in terms of the goods they can purchase, they are less well off. Hence, they supply less labour and hence output at the new level of prices, P_1. The SAS curve, therefore, shifts to the left and towards a new equilibrium at C. The path of adjustment may not be smooth, however, and could well involve overshooting if expectations do not adjust smoothly. In this case, the movement of output might be as indicated in Figure 2.8.

In this scenario, expansions of aggregate demand are destabilizing and produce cycles in output. Monetarists, therefore, advocate that the expansion of the money supply should merely accommodate the underlying long-term growth rate of real output in the economy as set by productivity increases. The essence of their position is that such growth can only occur in the long run because of a shift in the LAS curve and that these shifts occur independently of demand.

It is perhaps worth looking at the reverse case (Figure 2.7). Given the monetarist position, a reduction in AD from AD_1 to AD_0 should move the economy from C to D in the short run and to A in the long run.

Critics would argue that the long run may be very long and that the movement from D to A can be speeded up by government policy changes. They also point out that the money supply is difficult to control, even on an annual basis.

New classical

The new classical school (NC) may be regarded as extreme monetarist. There are two elements in the approach of its adherents. First, they believe that economic agents will make efficient use of all available information about the variable about which expectations are formed. They are assumed to act as if they used a model (in their heads) for forecasting and these forecasts formed the basis of their expectations (about the exchange rate or prices, for example). Hence their expectations are consistent with the predictions of their (own) macro model. These are called 'rational expectations' (RE). Thus, if people believe that a change in the money supply affects the price level, they will use information on the money supply to predict prices. The second strand in their argument is that all prices are perfectly flexible so that markets (e.g. goods and the foreign exchange (FOREX) market) clear in all periods immediately. These two elements taken together imply a much sharper process of adjustment than for orthodox monetarism (when a credible policy change is announced in advance).

Note, however, that RE can also be applied in models where prices are sluggish (sticky) and these models do not produce the 'extreme' NC results described below. We take up sticky price RE models in Chapter 6 when discussing exchange rate overshooting.

The essence of the NC position can be illustrated by assuming, for example, that the government announces a higher money supply target for next year (i.e. an anticipated change) and that this is indicated by the shift in AD from AD_0 to AD_1 in Figure 2.7. Economic agents know that the increase in the money supply is to occur and also know that this will affect prices and produce a new equilibrium at C. As they are 'rational', they immediately adjust expectations and we move straight from A to C.

In this scenario, there are no short-run effects on output from an anticipated change in the money supply. On the other hand, even the NC school recognizes that an unanticipated increase in the money supply will have effects on output in the very short run. This is because suppliers of output are 'surprised' by the price increase and see that more sales are temporarily profitable at the higher prices (but fixed wages) and hence expand output (along SAS_0 in Figure 2.8). However, this move from AB is either very quickly reversed if the money supply falls back to its original level or the economy quickly moves to C if the increase in the money supply turns out to be permanent. The NC school, therefore, makes a clear distinction between the effects of anticipated and unanticipated changes in policy variables.

Note that the authorities cannot keep on randomly increasing the money supply to expand output. Rational agents will recognize this fact and the (initially unanticipated) increase will become anticipated and then it will affect only prices and not output.

An important point about NC is that it seems to offer two simple solutions to inflation. If the rate of inflation is considered too high, all that needs to be done is to announce a reduction in the money supply that must be credible (i.e. believed by agents).

If expectations adjust immediately there will be no effects on output. Thus in static terms a cut in AD from AD_1 to AD_0 (Figure 2.7) immediately takes us from C to a new price level of P_0 at point A. Of crucial importance here, of course, is the credibility of the announcement. Thus some NC protagonists favour 'cold turkey' (i.e. a large announced cut in the money supply) rather than the orthodox monetarist gradualist approach. The former, it is argued, has more impact on expectations because it is a clear break with a previous policy stance.

In addition to the criticisms of orthodox monetarism it may be argued against NC/rational expectations that:

1 most people have neither the knowledge nor the economic expertise to be rational (although we only require those 'on the margin' to be rational for the theory to be valid);
2 expectations are slow to adjust because agents must learn about their new environment and RE has no model of learning behaviour; and
3 some prices are 'sticky'; thus, although the NC approach may be

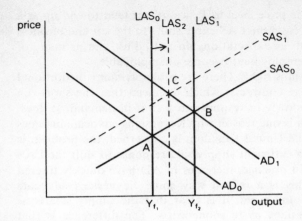

Figure 2.9 A Keynesian view

usefully applied to financial and FOREX markets, it should not be applied to labour and goods markets.

Keynesian

The essence of the Keynesian position is that instability is endemic to capitalist economies and that the manipulation of aggregate demand is needed to prevent recurrent crises. Furthermore, aggregate demand and supply are not independent and there may be no automatic adjustment to full employment. Again, Figure 2.7 may be used to illustrate the latter Keynesian views. Assume that we begin at point A with output Y_f and that policy-makers wish to expand output. Thus they use monetary or fiscal policy to shift AD from AD_0 to AD_1 and we again move to point B on SAS_0. The problem is to stay there and Keynesians would argue that if the economy can be held long enough at B the LAS would begin to shift to the right. This could be because the higher levels of demand would increase business confidence, investment and the productivity of the economy so that potential output was higher. Thus, increases in aggregate demand may generate an appropriate supply response. The simplest case would be the situation depicted in Figure 2.9 and a permanent movement to point B. In practice, the short-run supply curve would also probably shift and the LAS curve might not shift as far as B so that a more realistic result would be point C on SAS_1 and LAS_2.

It should be emphasized that this applies in reverse, too. Thus, if we begin at point C in Figure 2.7 with an employment level Y_f and attempt to reduce the price level to P_0 we in fact tend to end up at a point like D. In this case, the LAS curve shifts to the left and business confidence is eroded, as expectations do not adjust and as many of those tainted by unemployment become unemployable.

So are the Keynesians right? There are probably many institutional factors (such as wage contracts) which do mean that the short-run supply curve shifts slowly in response to a shift in demand. It does, however, shift which is one reason why Keynesians advocate incomes policies. As far as the United Kingdom is concerned, the problem is also one of getting a sufficient supply-side response to shift the LAS curve to the right. In practice, increases in AD have quickly filtered into imports and this is a reason why some Keynesians advocate import controls. In any event, it is clear that the supply side is as important to Keynesians as to monetarists. The difference is that manipulation of demand is also important in the Keynesian case.

2.3   CONCLUSION

There are, then, a number of important differences among groups of economists as to how the economy operates. The important differences concern the use of rational expectations, the operation of the supply side of the economy and whether an increase in aggregate demand is needed to boost that supply side. Although there has been a narrowing of differences in recent years, with Keynesians, in particular, accepting the importance of supply-side policies to boost economic growth, substantial differences remain as will be evident in subsequent chapters.

3 Risk and its impact on business

3.1 THE BUSINESS CYCLE

General trading conditions can have an important effect on the viability of individual enterprises, as the events of 1979–81 and 1990–1 have dramatically shown in the UK manufacturing sector. Such trading conditions are indicated by the business or trade cycle that typically charts the movement of real output around its trend value. Given the extent of interdependency in world markets, the business cycle usually affects all market-based industrial countries more or less simultaneously and indeed many less industrialized ones, too. Nevertheless, there can be differences in the impact, scale and precise timing of the cycle in particular economies reflecting a range of specific domestic influences. Figure 3.1, which gives details of the business cycle for the seven major OECD economies, demonstrates these points. Notice, for example, how the oil crisis of the early 1970s caused a major dip in GDP in all seven. Notice also how the austere monetary policies of Mrs Thatcher's UK government caused a dramatic fall in UK industrial production relative to trends in 1980.

As can also be seen from Figure 3.1, all seven countries have clearly suffered from short-run cycles lasting from four to eight years in length, a situation that seems to be endemic to industrial societies.

In the United Kingdom, an aggregate measure of the trade cycle is used, the so-called 'coincident' indicator, and this is based on the movement of six variables. These are the three alternative estimates of GDP (income, output and expenditure), the index of manufacturing production, the index of volume of retail sales, and CBI industrial trends survey information on changes in stocks of materials used in production and on the number of firms working at below capacity.

Throughout the nineteenth century and up to the Second World War fluctuations in economic activity were dramatic, involving

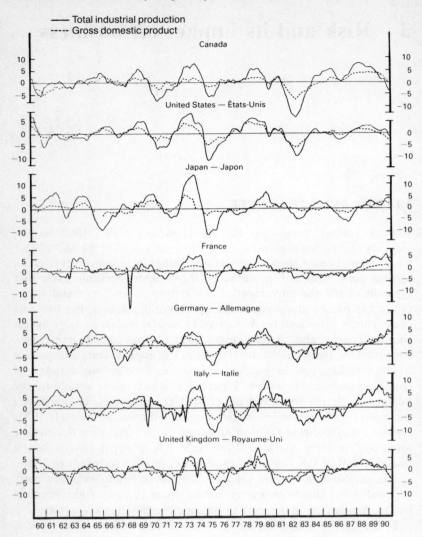

Figure 3.1 Cycles in industrial production and GDP
Source: OECD (1991) *Historical Statistics*

significant falls in output from time to time. In the United Kingdom, for example, downturns occurred in 1907–9, 1921–4, 1926–7 and, of course, in the Great Depression after 1929. The period from the end of the War to the early 1970s was, however, unique in that during that time recession meant a fall in the growth of output as opposed to a fall in absolute real value. Since 1974, the pre-War pattern has been re-established involving falling output and, as in the mid-1980s and early 1990s, significant increases in unemployment.

Figure 3.2 details the United Kingdom business cycle since 1971 and if we examine the 'coincident' indicator it can be seen that the country has experienced minor cycles of between four and five years in length. What is clear, however, is that the deviation from trend has recently been increasing and this explains the revival of interest in long swings. To some, the deviation from trend is explained by the fact that long swings are superimposed on the short ones. However, there are few observations of a fifty-year cycle and so far no accepted theoretical explanation for its existence. If an explanation for the long cycle does exist, it may lie with exogenous factors such as population changes, the accumulation of new inventions, the opening up of new territories and changing patterns of trade between developed and undeveloped countries (Rostow 1978). If these factors are crucial then the existence of long waves of similar duration may be largely coincidental. Either way, there is not doubt about the existence of short cycles and what these demonstrate is the risk and uncertainty involved in business. A new investment, for example, may succeed or fail depending on whether it is launched at the start of an upturn or a downturn in the cycle.

3.2   RISK AND THE INDIVIDUAL BUSINESS

The problem may perhaps be emphasized by showing the real difficulties involved in investment appraisal as opposed to the neat solutions suggested by the financial textbooks. Assume, for example, that the firm uses the net present value (NPV) method of appraisal and that it is considering investing in new plant to produce its product, steel ingots. The formula for the NPV is as follows:

$$NPV = A_0 + \frac{A_1}{(1 + r)^1} + \frac{A_2}{(1 + r)^2} + \ldots + \frac{A_n}{(1 + r)^n}$$

where A_0 is the initial capital outlay; A_1 to A_n are the net returns to the project in years 1 to n (i.e. receipts less running costs and any additional capital costs); and r is the rate of interest.

In practice, the solution to the problem is far from simple. What the

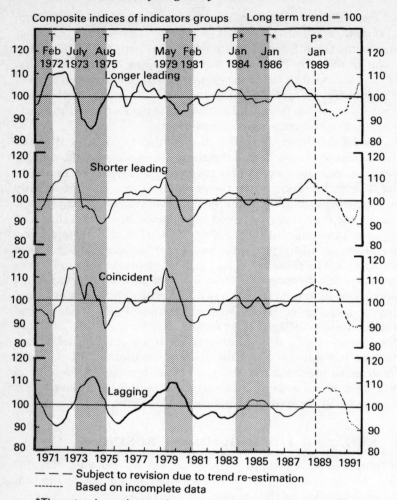

Figure 3.2 Cyclical indicators
Source: Central Statistical Office (1991) *Economic Trends* 457

Table 3.1 NPV given various assumptions

States of the world		Interest rate	
		10% (0.6)	13% (0.4)
Growth of GDP	3% (0.5)	£10,000	£4,000
	−1% (0.5)	−£1,000	−£4,000

returns will be in various years it is hard to predict. Quite apart from such factors as what domestic competitor firms are doing, it will depend on such influences as the level of aggregate demand in the economy and the demand for steel in particular, and this in turn is likely to be influenced by such factors as prices and exchange rates. These, in turn, will be influenced by the macroeconomic policies of governments around the world and by the supply-side characteristics and performance of a large number of countries. Moreover, inflation will influence nominal cash receipts. But the problem does not finish here. If firms choose to borrow funds as the project unfolds, there is the additional problem of which interest rate to use as a discount factor. Rates of interest change significantly over the life of projects, so this is a far from easy problem to solve. In any event, it is compounded by the existence of inflation, expectations of which will be incorporated in nominal interest rates.

The standard way to allow for such influences is to consider a range of outcomes based upon different assumptions. Meaningful figures in terms of expected outcomes can only be calculated, however, if probabilities can be attached to alternative outcomes. A simple analysis is shown in Table 3.1.

If the probabilites are shown in parentheses then the expected outcome is:

$$(10,000 \times 0.6 \times 0.5) + (4,000 \times 0.4 \times 0.5) + (-1,000 \times 0.6 \times 0.5)$$
$$+ (-4,000 \times 0.4 \times 0.5) = £2,700$$

There is an expected profit of £2,700 in the case shown in Table 3.1. In practice, however, there are many influences and many outcomes, while insurance-type situations where the risks are known or can be calculated are rare. The entrepreneur, therefore, must subjectively decide whether and when to invest and in what way, given the best information he can obtain of likely future events.

3.3   ENVIRONMENTAL INFLUENCES

It will be obvious, of course, that many of the environmental influences affecting the above investment decision also affect other aspects of decision-taking in the individual enterprise. Clearly, the importance of these influences to a particular firm will depend upon the nature of its business and they may differ in importance at different points in time. What influences then can be identified?

The economic environment

This is clearly of great importance and is the primary concern of this book. Of significance are such factors as the level of world and domestic trade as evidenced by the trade cycle. Also of concern are the exchange rate, which will clearly affect the competitiveness of exports and imports, the level of interest rates and the availability of credit.

The government

Political decisions are, of course, related to the economic environment as much of policy is economic in direction. Thus, the decision in the United Kingdom to adopt monetarist principles in the late 1970s did much to raise interest rates and influence the movement of the sterling exchange rate. This made British manufacturing industry uncompetitive in the early 1980s but strengthened the role of the City of London.

However, there are a great many other policy decisions that have an impact on business. The government, for example, often adopts a regulatory role in setting safety standards, maximum hours of work, minimum wage levels, quality specifications, granting of patents and so on, all of which may have specific effects on particular areas of business. In some cases, these are supplemented by international law or, in the case of Europe, by the European Commission.

Moreover, government decisions on pay in the public sector also affect business for comparability reasons. Similarly, the financing of pay deals in the public sector and of public expenditure generally affects levels of business taxation and, therefore, profitability. The latter may also be affected if the government competes with the private sector for the best employees or for investment funds.

A further important government influence is exercised through the purchase of the output of the private sector. Particular firms are greatly affected by whether they are successful in obtaining the often huge government contracts and by the systems of contracting adopted. Defence, in particular, is one area where specific companies have benefited from large orders and the technical expertise involved in fulfilling them. Other political influences concern both industrial and employment policy and these may have a differential effect on different firms and/or different industrial areas.

Capital markets

We have already mentioned the importance of interest rates and will be returning to this in due course. Also of importance, however, are the attitudes of financial institutions to different types of business. It is often argued that it is more difficult to obtain venture capital in the United Kingdom than in other developed countries, particularly for small firms, and that as a result many British inventions are developed abroad. It is also argued that United Kingdom financial institutions have much more of an 'arms length' approach to industry than is the case, for example, in Germany where lending banks often hold large equity shareholdings in industrial companies and exercise voting rights. All this may affect the types of business that can attract funds and, therefore, the direction of economic development.

The labour market

It has already been argued that the recruitment policies of the government and its negotiations on levels of pay will have clear spill-over effects on the private sector. Similarly, decisions in one part of the private sector will have repercussions in another, for in many cases industries and the firms that comprise them are essentially competing for the same labour force. Recent years have hardly been characterized by general labour shortages, but at other times these have been important constraints on the level of output growth. Even now there are shortages of particular types of labour, such as electronics engineers, which are a severe constraint on the growing high technology industries. The problem is that the better qualified labour is required to be, the more difficult it is to redress labour shortages, for it takes a great deal of education and educational planning to increase the output of electronics engineers. In some cases, it is necessary to change the attitudes of prospective employees and educational institutions in favour of subjects that may not traditionally have been taught or chosen to a sufficient extent. A further problem is that, given the pace of technical change, a particular educational investment may turn out to be obsolete even before it is completed.

Cultural and social attitudes will, of course, also be important in conditioning the supply of entrepreneurs on the one hand and labour relations on the other, both of which will be important influences on the level and type of business activity. Finally, cultural attitudes, educational standards and levels of remuneration in other countries will all affect the labour market in any one country such as the United Kingdom.

The level of technology

The events of the last two hundred years in the United Kingdom provide ample evidence of the importance of technological developments in business life. In the early years of industrialization, it was inventions in the textile and iron industries that gave a major boost to the United Kingdom economy. With the ending of the age of steam, however, and the introduction of oil-based technology much of British industrial production became inefficient and / or obsolete. The process has continued in recent years where industries based on electronics have been a major feature of growth in countries such as Japan. Indeed, improvements in communications and budgetary control techniques, together with technological improvements on the production side, have enabled firms to differentiate their production activities from their head office functions. Little wonder then that much of production has been decentralized to low wage regions and low wage countries, and only head offices have been retained in cities such as London, New York and Paris.

Suppliers

At the macro scale, firms dependent upon raw material imports will clearly be adversely affected by a depreciating exchange rate. The latter might reflect decisions in a particular important economy such as the USA or decisions by a body such as OPEC to raise the price of oil. Equally, movements in the exchange rate could reflect the economic performance of particular countries or the over-exploitation of particular sources of supply.

Indeed, supplies are of crucial importance to any firm, particularly if the number of alternative sources is limited. Linkages between firms in a modern economy are so complex that a strike in one supplier may directly and indirectly affect a large number of businesses. There are many examples of businesses being forced to close by events with which they were not directly involved.

Customers

Moving to the demand side, it is, of course, crucial that firms understand their market and changes in the market environment. One aspect of this is that firms or potential entrepreneurs must be aware of gaps in the market that exist or can be created and must seek to fill them. Another aspect is that firms must monitor the demand for existing products and methods of producing them so that they can remain competitive. This brings us to a further important influence, that of competitors.

Competitors

In this respect, the firm in a particular market will be affected by the decisions of existing firms in the same market and by the potential entry of others. As far as existing competitors are concerned, there will be a need to monitor all operations including price, marketing, cost, methods of production, relationships with suppliers, vertical and horizontal integration and so on. For potential entrants monitoring may be more difficult. The existing firm will need to be aware of any entry barriers that exist in the industry such as economies of scale, consumer goodwill and legal protection, and of any threats to those barriers. In the case of legal protection this may come from changes in policy so that lobbying of government may be important. On the technical side, it is a case of being aware of new developments that may threaten existing markets. This may concern new production methods favouring either larger or smaller firms in the same industry or indeed developments in other industries that may make firms in those industries potential competitors in one's own. Thus, for example, the development of UPVC made producers of plastics competitors in the building supplies industry.

Sociocultural influences

It has been argued (Weiner 1981) that cultural attitudes may have been important in the relative economic decline of the United Kingdom and they have been suggested as important in the modern growth of Japan. As far as differences between countries are concerned, these may affect the decisions of, for example, multinational companies as to where they site plant and this may have implications for economic development and prosperity. As for individual countries, we have already argued that sociocultural attitudes will affect risk-taking and entrepreneurship, and it is this that Thatcherism attempted to improve in the United Kingdom. At the general level attitudes are certainly slow to change, but change they do and firms have to be aware of this. An example is provided by the Campaign for Real Ale, which curtailed the plans of the big United Kingdom brewers to move towards exclusively mass-produced keg beer.

3.4   THE CHANGING ENVIRONMENT

There are then a number of environmental influences and although they have been itemized separately they are, of course, interrelated. Many government decisions, for example, are a response to changes in the economic and sociocultural environment. As far as the economic environment is concerned, many governments reacted to inflation by adopting monetarist policies. Some have adopted protectionism in the face of economic recession. As for the sociocultural environment, government must react to changing public attitudes. A case in point is smoking, which has become increasingly prohibited as it has become increasingly unacceptable socially and this has affected the tobacco industry and the places dependent upon it.

But firms too are forced to adapt directly to changes in social attitudes. An example is provided by the impact of EC legislation concerning the constituents of food products, which has increasingly drawn public attention to the use of additives. Concern that some of these additives may be toxic has affected demand and many manufacturers have now cut down on the use of these and/or swapped non-harmful for harmful ones.

Indeed, the problem for business is that all the above environmental influences not only interact but change frequently and sometimes significantly. Manufacturing firms in the United Kingdom have, for example, been dramatically affected by the effect of North Sea oil on the exchange rate, the entry of the United Kingdom into the EC and the adoption by the government of monetarist principles. They have also been affected by, and have themselves conditioned, educational decisions, decisions that have increasingly favoured areas such as business studies, accountancy and engineering.

Similarly, firms in all developed countries have been and are being affected by the increased use of microelectronics and information technology. There are, of course, many other examples of environmental change, such as greater concern for green issues, and its significance suggests that firms need a strategy to deal with it.

3.5 STRATEGY FOR RISK

It would, of course, be possible to write a whole book on environmental uncertainty and strategies to deal with it. For our purposes it is sufficient to refer the reader to the growing literature on business policy (e.g. Johnson and Scholes 1990) and to present a summary of the issues.

A strategy is really required both:

1 to reduce the level of uncertainty; and
2 to manage the impact of undesirable change.

It terms of the first aspect, one approach is for the firm to secure supplies and markets either through long-term purchasing agreements or by vertical integration. Similarly, the firm can attempt to ensure a market by creating conditions in which it is difficult for new firms to enter its industry. These include advertising, the use of brand names, the utilization of economies of scale and the creation of absolute cost advantages.

As for the second aspect, the impact of change can be managed by improved perception by the firm of the existence of risk and of the crucial factors affecting it. One solution is to improve the adaptability of an organization; the recent movement towards franchising and subcontracting may be seen as evidence that large firms have been active in this respect. Also important, of course, is diversification and this is true of a number of areas.

Farmers do not wish to be dependent upon individual crops, the return on which may rely upon such diverse influences as the vagaries of the weather or political infighting in the EC. Similarly, it has been argued that firms in science-based industries with fast rates of technical change have to be very large so that successes can offset the inevitable failures (Pratten 1990). The predominance of industrial conglomerates is evidence of the philosophy of 'don't keep all your eggs in one basket'.

An economic strategy

Whatever strategy is used at the micro level, the businessman will still be affected by general macroeconomic changes. What, therefore, does he do in this respect? The most important strategy is for the businessman to improve his knowledge of the likely course of economic events.

At the simplest level, the businessman can make use of cyclical indicators, four of which are shown in Figure 3.2. Leading indicators are those that precede and signal changes in the economy generally. Thus, in the United Kingdom, a long leading indicator is composed of the *Financial Times* (FT) share index and evidence on housing starts and business confidence. A shorter leading indicator is based on such evidence as new car registrations, company profits and changes in industrial demand. However, as will be obvious, these factors will already be influencing and influenced by a large number of businesses before they are published and therefore their usefulness is limited. One way around the problem is for businessmen to extrapolate trends, but since the cycle is of irregular length this is unlikely to be practicable. The alternative is to use economic forecasts and/or some form of scenario planning.

A second major aspect of economic strategy is the use of forward markets. These set a price 'today' for future delivery of goods (e.g. wheat) or financial assets (e.g. foreign exchange). This allows firms to hedge against future changes in 'spot' prices by making a contract with the price set 'today'. Speculators often adopt a middle role and by matching buyers and sellers usually ensure that forward markets work efficiently. Given the increasing internationalization of production and financial markets, it is hardly surprising that forward markets are very important features of dealing in both money and commodities.

A third possibility is the use of a portfolio of assets, both financial and tangible. In this respect, firms may be compared with individuals in that they spread risks by having a portfolio of industrial shares and other financial assets. Some of these may be high risk in that they rise or fall faster than the stock market index, some are low risk in that they tend to rise or fall slower than the market and some move in the opposite direction to the market. Increasingly, assets are held internationally, which is a further method of reducing risk. One aspect of this portfolio diversification is that firms may undertake production in a number of countries, thus switching production between various plants depending on local cost conditions. A good example here are multinational car firms, where parts of the same car can be made in different countries.

It is these elements of planning and minimizing risk from changes in the macroeconomy that form the major part of this book and we now examine them in some detail. We begin with a look at economic forecasting.

4   The use of forecasts

It was argued in Chapter 3 that one of the major methods of reducing risk as far as the macroeconomic environment is concerned was to use economic forecasts to anticipate the future. In practice, of course, this is far more difficult than it sounds.

The problem is that there are a large number of forecasts, differing to a greater or lesser degree from each other and covering a large number of variables. As far as the United Kingdom is concerned, most businessmen will be aware that the Treasury produces forecasts, but there are, in addition, ten other major institutional forecasting bodies including the National Institute of Economic and Social Research (NIESR), the London Business School (LBS), the OECD, the European Community, the CBI and some universities. There are also a number of City firms in the forecasting game including Phillips and Drew, Goldman Sachs, James Capel, Barclays, County Nat West and the Midland Bank. This adds up to a large amount of diverse and often conflicting information for the businessman to assess.

A flavour of what is involved may be gained by looking at a range of sample forecasts as depicted in Table 4.1. These refer to the year 1990 and were made at various times in the early part of that year. They only relate to some of the variables included in the forecasts and even here comparision is complicated by differences in variable definition and inclusion, and occasionally by slight differences in the time period to which the forecasts on individual variables relate.

4.1   FORECAST DIFFERENCES

There are substantial differences between the three main forecasts listed. This conclusion is reinforced by examining the fifth and sixth columns, which give the maximum and minimum projections of the twelve, main, non-City forecasts. How then can the businessman

Table 4.1 Comparison of forecasts for 1990 (percentage change on previous year[1])

Variable	Treasury March 1990	Forecast and date NIESR Feb. 1990	LBS Feb. 1990	Average	Spread of forecast projections[3] Low	High	Actual
1 GDP	1.0	1.4	1.0	1.3	0.6	2.7	0.5
2 Private consumption	1.25	1.7	1.1	1.3	0.4	2.1	1.0
3 Government expenditure	0.25	0.9	0.3	0.9	-1.2	3.5	1.75
4 Gross fixed investment	-1.25	-2.8	-0.1	-0.5	-10	3.2	1.75
5 Export	7.25	7.95	8.5	7.6	4.0	8.5	4.75
6 Imports	1.0	0.8	1.5	1.2	-1.1	3.4	1.5
7 RPI	7.25	6.8	6.8	7.1	3.8	8.0	10.0
8 Average earnings	–	9.3	8.9	9.2	7.6	9.7	9.5
9 Adult unemployment (millions)	–	1.63	1.72	1.72	1.6	1.8	1.6
10 World trade	6.0	5.3	4.7	5.7	4.6	6.9	5.0
11 PSBR[2]	-7.0	-11.9	-11.3	-8.6	-13.5	-5.9	-0.75

Source: HM Treasury (1990) Comparison of outside forecasts and CSO (1991) Economic Trends 449
Notes:
1 Except unemployment; occasionally changes are for slightly different periods. It should be emphasized that there are differences in the definition of variables.
2 PSBR = public sector borrowing requirement. These figures relate to the financial year 1990–1.
3 These figures apply to twelve major non-City forecasts.

Table 4.2 Forecast performance 1990[1]

Variable	Best	Worst
GDP	TR/LBS	NIESR
Private consumption	LBS	NIESR
Government expenditure	NIESR	TR
Gross fixed investment	TR	LBS
Exports	TR	LBS
Imports	LBS	NIESR
RPI	TR	NIESR/LBS
Average earnings	NIESR	LBS
Adult unemployment	NIESR	LBS
World trade	NIESR/LBS	TR
PSBR	TR	LBS

Note:
1 LBS = London Business School; NIESR = National Institute of Economic and Social Research; TR = HM Treasury.

interpret this bewildering amount of information? One alternative is to ignore it altogether, a course of action that on some occasions would have been justified by the extremely poor performance of the forecasters in general. Most of them, for example, failed to predict the severity and speed of the UK recession in the second half of 1990. The UK Treasury was particularly heavily criticized, having been forced to revise its forecasts for 1991 from a growth of 0.5 per cent predicted in November 1990 to a fall of 2 per cent predicted in March 1991.

Nevertheless, there are long periods over which the forecasters have done better so that in some such circumstances their output may be considered preferable to the uninformed guesses of individual businessmen. How then should the businessman proceed?

One alternative would be to use the forecasts of those forecasting bodies that have done well in the past. Ranking forecasts in this way turns out, however, to be far more difficult than it might appear. This is easily demonstrated by ranking our forecasts for 1990 by comparing the forecast output with what actually happened, as shown in the final column of Table 4.1. Table 4.2 summarizes the performance of the three major forecasts listed. What is clear is that there is no forecast that performs best for all variables. Indeed, the top and bottom prizes seem to be well shared out.

This is clearly a snapshot of a few variables at a point in time and what is really required is a detailed analysis of forecast performance relative to many variables over a long time period. Most forecasters do, in fact, assess the performance of their own forecasts and some, including the National Institute, compare some of the major ones.

Nevertheless, it appears at present that a long-period detailed assessment is still lacking, although a start has been made by the macroeconomics modelling bureau of the University of Warwick. This produces an annual assessment of models (e.g. Wallis *et al.* 1987). There are clear difficulties of course, given definitional differences and the large numbers of variables involved. A major additional factor is that the models from which the forecasts are developed are themselves adapted over time as the forecasters try to improve their performance (Wallis *et al.* 1987, Keating 1985a).

It is these types of difficulty that also confront the businessman in trying to rank the forecasts. Our assessment is that while some forecasters possibly do perform badly for long periods, among the others different forecasters do best at different times. Finally, it clearly depends on which forecast variable we are dealing with, so that there are no easy answers. We, therefore, now turn to a second possible course of action, which is to use a consensus forecast for business purposes. Although there is no mathematical reason for an average of forecasts to outperform an individual forecasting team, there is some long-term evidence to suggest that, in practice, it tends to do so. Even so, the average does not rank well on the basis of the 1990 evidence from Table 4.1.

This leaves us with a third possibility, which is for the businessman to understand the differences between forecasts in order to have some rational basis for choosing between them. Why then do forecasts differ?

4.2 UNDERSTANDING THE DIFFERENCES

There are, in fact, a number of main reasons why forecasts differ:

1 there may be differences in the information available to forecasters;
2 there may be differences in the judgement exercised in adjusting equation residuals and constants;
3 there may be different expectations of the movement of exogenous variables (i.e. those not estimated within the forecasting model); and
4 the models themselves may differ in structure.

To demonstrate these points, consider a simple Keynesian textbook model:

$$[Y_t = C_t + G_t] \tag{4.1}$$

$$C_t = a + bY_t + u_t \qquad o < b < l \tag{4.2}$$

where Y_t = output (GDP); C_t = consumers' expenditure; G_t = government expenditure; and u_t is a zero-mean random error term. The value of the multiplier k is obtained from the solution of (4.1) and (4.2):

$$Y_t = \frac{a}{1-b} + \frac{G_t}{1-b} + \frac{U_t}{1-b} = K(a + G_t + u_t)$$

(4.3)

and $k = 1/(1-b)$. The multiplier measures the impact on Y of a unit change in G. In this simple model, it is determined by the size of the marginal propensity to consume out of income, i.e. b. The larger b is, the larger is the multiplier.

Forecasts of output by two rival forecasting bodies may differ in this case because:

1 of different assumptions about the future course of the exogenous variable, government expenditure;
2 a different value is assumed for the marginal propensity to consume, b (this is usually described as a difference in the structure of the model);
3 different 'add factors', (residual u_t or intercept adjustments) are used to take account of 'special factors' expected to operate in the future or to account for the fact that recent values of u_t, the error term, are not random (but, for example, have all recently been positive). Such adjustments are sometimes referred to as 'tender, loving care'; and
4 the coefficient, a, could represent 'other' influences on consumption such as interest rates. Forecasting teams differ over what variables to include in an equation as well as the size of their impact.

In practice, the models differ in structure for a whole variety of reasons and we now examine this issue in some detail.

The models, like the economy itself, are extremely complex. They are macroeconomic models that give a mathematical representation of the quantitative relationships between such variables as employment, output, consumption, investment, prices, interest rates and exchange rates. A large number of equations are involved, including both identities reflecting the national income accounting framework and behavioural equations that describe the aggregate actions of consumers, producers, investors and so on. The numerical values of the parameters in the behavioural equations are usually determined by statistical estimation from historical data.

The construction of economy-wide models has developed over the last thirty years, facilitated by data improvements and advances in econometric techniques and computer technology (Wallis *et al.* 1987). The models themselves change over time in response to such influences as developments in theory, empirical evidence, performance and institutional arrangements.

Nevertheless, the philosophies of the model builders change relatively slowly, so that the models have continuing differences in terms of their characteristics. Let us look briefly at the characteristics of the models represented by the three forecasts in Table 4.1. Further details are given in Chapter 9, in Wallis *et al.* (1987), Keating (1985a) and in the regular newsletters of the ESRC Modelling Bureau of the University of Warwick.

4.3   THE MODELS

The Treasury model

This is one of the largest of the United Kingdom quarterly models, with around 385 equations and 500 variables. It is eclectic, being a mixture of Keynesian and monetarist elements. The Keynesian view that changes in policy variables influence output as well as price holds, but the model also has monetarist characteristics. In certain cases, for example, fiscal policy has no effect on output in the long run (crowding out) while a change in the money supply can result in higher inflation and little or no change in real output (i.e. neutrality of money).

The NIESR model

This is a quarterly model with 176 behavioural equations and 386 variables. The model originated as a standard Keynesian income–expenditure model, but in recent years has been adapted to include supply-side influences including rational expectations. It can only now be described as standard Keynesian in the specific sense that short-term fluctuations in output are mainly determined by changes in aggregate demand.

The London Business School model

This is also quarterly and covers over 100 behavioural equations and over 700 variables. Although again based on the income–expenditure framework it has, like the Treasury and NIESR models, a number of monetarist characteristics. Recent versions of the LBS model have included a detailed model of the financial system and the determination of interest rates. This type of 'portfolio model' is discussed further in Chapter 7.

There are, then, important differences between the above three models, which are among the largest in the UK. Others are much smaller, such as the Liverpool quarterly model which is neo-classical in terms of foundation and has fewer than twenty behavioural equations and only around fifty variables in total.

So, where does this leave our businessman? He now understands why forecasts differ and he must come to some conclusion as to which forecast to believe. Clearly, like the rest of us, he will have his own opinions regarding the underlying relationships outlined above and if he himself believes in monetarism may choose a monetarist forecast as his guide.

Our own view is that the experience of the United Kingdom economy over the last decade gives little support to the new classical view, although expectations are clearly now recognized as more important than hitherto, particularly in financial markets. However, some prices do appear 'sticky', contrary to the new classical view. Although money is clearly an important influence on economic variables, it is difficult to measure (viz. M1, MO, M3, M4 definitions of money in the United Kingdom), many of the monetarist predictions have not been borne out and monetary prescriptions do not seem to have worked as well as advocates argued at the outset. Keynesians have been forced to adapt their position and now recognize the importance of interest rates as well as fiscal policy in influencing output and inflation. Nevertheless, there is still no consensus and no consensus forecast. The businessman must, therefore, interpret the forecasts in relation to his own beliefs regarding both the nature of economic relationships and the future course of key economic events. Indeed, with the increasing cost-effectiveness of personal computers and the compatibility of existing models with a variety of computers, the day is rapidly approaching when the businessman can quickly produce his own forecasts using rival models (e.g. London Business School, Liverpool and National Institute models are now available on IBM PC-compatible micros). He can also check the sensitivity of forecasts to alternative assumptions – an issue to which we now turn.

The sensitivity of forecasts

Most economic forecasters know that their forecasts will turn out to be incorrect. One reason is that they are conditional on prior assumptions about, for example, future government expenditure, tax and monetary policy, which can be only imperfectly known at the time the forecast is made. A second is that they are based on estimates of recent economic indicators, estimates that in due course often turn out to have been wrong.

Irrespective of the reasons, however, the fact that forecasts are often wrong, as demonstrated by the data of Table 4.1, suggests that the businessman, if he uses such forecasts, would be wise to do so with caution. One approach would be for him to conduct his own sensitivity analysis of a central forecast, based on his view of what are the major uncertainties for the future, using a central forecast that can be produced on a personal computer (e.g. an IBM-compatible machine, see National Institute 1987, London Business School 1987). By way of an example, suppose the businessman feels that the publicly available forecasts are too pessimistic on the outlook for world trade as he has 'inside' marketing information from his sales force and overseas subsidiaries. All he has to do is to put in his set of figures for world trade and the model will produce (usually graphically) the difference between the central forecast and the businessman's 'new' forecast. The advantage in using the computer model is that it is likely to embody all the main 'feedbacks' in the economy. For example, higher world trade directly boosts exports, but may lead to an appreciation in the exchange rate and some loss in price competitiveness which will attenuate export growth. The impact of export growth in the domestic market (via the multiplier) and on domestic prices will also be printed out by the model's solution programme. Hence the businessman can assess the impact of his alternative assumptions about overseas demand on domestic demand and domestic cost and price inflation. If he is willing to repeat the exercise for alternative scenarios, he can apply the rules of decision-making under uncertainty (e.g. maximin, expected values) to rank his options (Lumby 1984).

Ideally, one would like to assess the sensitivity of a central forecast to changes in the parameters (e.g. the marginal propensity to consume, b) of the model – as well as to changes in exogenous variables (e.g. world trade or government expenditure). The former capability, however, is not yet widely available (because it may involve recompiling the model), but it is bound to become available in the near future. A possible feasible alternative is to use 'add factors' (residual or intercept adjustments) to approximate this effect.

4.4   SUMMARY

Although macroeconomic forecasts may be useful they should be used with care. One reason is that there are periods when the forecasters get things seriously wrong. A second is that there are many different forecasting institutions and there is no simple way of choosing between alternative models on the basis of past performance. Perhaps the most sensible thing for the businessman to do is to obtain a copy of his favoured model and use his own add factors (most of these may well be zero or constant, i.e. $u_t = O$, $u_t = \bar{u}$) to produce his own central forecast. He can then augment this with a sensitivity analysis based on different exogenous variable paths or different add-on factors. Computer technology is improving so rapidly that the businessman will soon be able quickly and easily to construct his own macro simulation model and use it for forecasting and sensitivity analysis.

A further interesting possibility is the development of disaggregated satellite models. The macro model may produce forecasts that are too aggregative for the businessman, for example, a forecast of total consumers' expenditure and aggregate personal incomes. However, the businessman may easily be able to base forecasts for his particular sectors on outputs from the aggregate forecast. For example, the businessman might construct (estimate) an equation for the demand for 'white goods' (e.g. washing machines, fridges, etc.) by consumers, based on aggregate incomes and the cost of borrowing. If the latter two variables appear as outputs of the main macro model, the impact of, say, government policy on the demand for white goods is easily accomplished by inputting the aggregate forecasts into the submodel.

5 The international environment 1
The influence of exchange rates on business

The international influences on business have become increasingly important over time and this process looks set to continue in the future. A number of influences have been important in this respect.

One important one is improvements in communications and budgetary control techniques, which have enabled manufacturing firms to differentiate their production activities from their head office functions. This has contributed to a great internationalization of production as firms have sought to take advantage of cheap sources of labour in, for example, the less developed countries.

Such internationalization of production has also occurred as firms have grown in size to become multinationals operating in many markets around the world, a process that has been fostered by the gradual abolition of tariff barriers and quotas through the 1960s and 1970s. Moreover, many service firms in, for example, banking, shipping, insurance and tourism operate in international markets and many in other fields are increasingly doing so. One reason for this is the link between manufacturing and services. There are clear advantages for a major UK manufacturing multinational in having, for example, the same firm of accountants or advertising consultants in London, New York and Sydney.

The liberation of exchange controls in many countries has also been an important influence in fostering the setting up of subsidiaries overseas and in the formation of international conglomerates in general. Many UK firms, such as BP and Unilever, have foreign subsidiaries and a large number of others are subsidiaries of foreign-based companies. Recent examples of foreign firms buying UK subsidiaries are the Austirlian brewing group Elders (owners of Courage) and the Swiss firm Nestlés (owners of Rowntree).

It is not only multinationals that have been affected by changes in the international environment, however. The expansion of demand in industrial countries and the increase in tourism have increased the demand for foreign goods. Thus firms such as Sainsbury in the UK now stock a far wider range of foreign drinks and foreign food than they did even a decade ago. There is, as a result, an increased willingness to accept 'foreign' goods and services in the UK generally, which means that even producers who buy inputs locally and sell their output in the domestic market are likely to be affected by foreign competition. Imports to the UK, for example, as a percentage of GDP (at factor cost and 1980 prices) increased from 24.4 in 1970 to 34.6 in 1987. Finally, it should be pointed out that not only has international trade become more important, but also the prices at which it has been carried out have become more volatile since the abolition of fixed exchange rates in 1972. This volatility can mean that there can be large swings in the value of a currency over quite short periods, swings that may not accurately reflect underlying economic conditions or fundamentals.

An example is provided by the US dollar, which fell from around 1.05$/£ early in 1985 to more than 1.40$/£ later in that year. It continued to fall subsequently to an average value of 1.64 in 1987 and to a value of 1.83 in March 1988.[1] Such movements in exchange rates can have very important effects on profitability of overseas sales and the cost of imported raw materials.

European exports of cars to the US, in particular, were badly affected by the falling dollar (i.e. rising Deutschmark, pound, and French franc exchange rates against the dollar). The dollar prices of West European cars rose in the USA by over a third from 1985–8 and, as a result, sales fell. In the first half of 1988, for example, US imports of these cars were 12 per cent lower than in the same period of 1987. Volvo, Porsche and Audi were among the hardest hit. Jaguar in the UK was also affected and, partly as a result, pre-tax profit fell from £121 million in 1986 to £97 million in 1987 (*Economist* 1988, *Independent* 1989).

5.1 THE IMPORTANCE OF EXCHANGE RATES

It appears, then, that movements of exchange rates are of great importance. Consider, for example, the case of a UK manufacturing firm that sells in the domestic and foreign markets and that buys in from abroad large quantities of raw materials, capital equipment and semi-finished products. Because of possible changes in exchange rates it will be difficult to forecast costs of production and the gains from holding stocks of inventories because costs in home country currency will be unpredictable. Equally, on the sales side, there may well be lead times between the date a contract is signed and the date of delivery when returns in foreign currency accrue. Thus, if our UK firm agrees to supply goods in three months' time to a US firm with the contract fixed in dollars, it may face substantial gains or losses in pounds sterling if the dollar–sterling exchange rate changes over the interval. Alternatively, if the UK firm prices its goods in sterling and sterling appreciates against the dollar, the firm may find that it loses its US sales.

An international firm also faces the possibility of exchange-rate risk if the firm is considering investing in overseas assets. These could be foreign government bonds, shares in foreign companies or fixed assets such as land and buildings. The problem now is that investment occurs today in the currency of the country in which the assets are to be purchased, while a stream of returns will occur in the future and which shareholders will require remitted in domestic currency.

Exchange risk is clearly then of considerable importance in modern business. How much the firm can do about it will partly depend upon its leverage over price, an issue to which we now turn.

5.2   PRICING AND OVERSEAS SALES

Homogeneous products

There are a number of well-developed, international 'spot' markets for homogeneous products such as the oil market in Rotterdam where prices are quoted in dollars. A UK firm selling in such a market has to sell at the prevailing international dollar price and in all probability can sell what it wants at that price. It, therefore, faces a horizontal demand curve or price line for its product. If so, the implications of a change in the $/£ exchange rate are straightforward. An appreciation in sterling results in a squeeze on domestic profit margins while a depreciation has the opposite effect. Take, for example, the case of a marginal North Sea oil field from which oil may be extracted at £8.57 per barrel. If the $/£ exchange rate is 1.75, this is a cost in dollar terms of $15. If the world market price of crude oil of the same quality is $18 a barrel, the profit margin is $3 per barrel. In sterling terms this is equal to $3/1.75 = £1.71$ which yields a profit margin over sterling cost of $1.71/8.57 = 19.6$ per cent. Now if sterling appreciates to 1.95$/£ and costs remain unchanged at £8.57 a barrel, then profit is squeezed to $18–16.7 = \$1.3$ a barrel. In sterling terms this means a return of just £0.66 per barrel, a rate of return on cost of only 7.8 per cent.

In practice, of course, there may be some offsetting reductions in

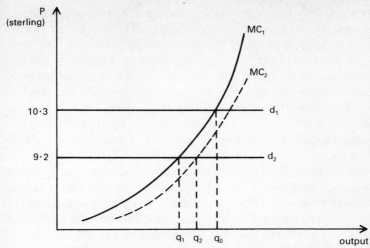

Figure 5.1 Output response of a UK oil exploration company to a change in the exchange rate and sterling price

cost if, for example, there is imported US equipment used on North Sea oil rigs or if the reduction in sterling import prices feeds through into retail prices and lower wage claims. The latter, however, might take a considerable time to work through.

What, then, will be the effects of these changes on UK oil firms? These are illustrated in Figure 5.1. The line d_1 shows the demand curve for a UK oil firm at a world price of \$18 and an exchange rate of 1.75\$/£ = £10.3 per barrel. The line d_2 shows the demand curve after the appreciation of sterling to 1.95 (\$/£); the sterling price is then 18/1.95 = £9.2 per barrel. The profit-maximizing firm will produce up to the point where revenue received per barrel equals the marginal cost of producing the last barrel. Thus, at price 10.3, output Q_0 is produced while at price 9.2, output is cut back to Q_1. If cost reductions then accrue because of the sterling appreciation, so that the marginal cost curve shifts to the right (=MC_2), output will rise to Q_2.

To sum up, the effect of an appreciation of sterling is a squeeze on the profit margins of those UK companies that must sell homogeneous products at the world market price. This, in turn, is likely to lead to output and employment contractions, at least in the short term.

Heterogeneous products

In practice most manufacturing (and service) firms produce output that is, to some extent, different from that of competitors. In such circumstances they face a downward-sloping demand curve because, as prices rise, brand loyalty ensures that not all customers are lost to rival firms with lower prices. What this means in practice is that firms have some discretion over the price they charge in both domestic and international markets. In the international context, an appreciation of the home country's exchange rate means that its products and services are now less competitive in world markets. But a UK firm, for example, selling a heterogeneous product (like a Jaguar car) can trade off volume changes against price changes as it does not lose all its market in the USA if it raises its dollar price.

The point is that, given the downward-sloping demand curve, it will now lose some sales but will be selling each unit at a higher dollar price. Indeed, total sterling revenue might decrease very little if foreign demand is sufficiently price inelastic. Suppose, for example, a UK firm is selling a sophisticated machine tool priced at £20,000 and, at an exchange rate of 1.75\$/£, this means a US price of \$35,000. Let us assume it sells a hundred at this price in the USA. If sterling now appreciates to 1.95\$/£, the UK manufacturer has two choices. The firm could still sell at the old dollar price of \$35,000, which will return only £17,949 per unit in home currency and clearly involves a significantly reduced profit margin. Alternatively, it could decide to raise the US price to, say, \$37,500 in the hope that it will not lose all its sales at this price. Assume sales fall to ninety-five, total dollar returns are \$3,562,500 which, in UK currency, is £1,826,923. This compares with an original sterling return of £2,000,000 before the exchange-rate change and one of £1,794,900 if option one had been taken. Clearly, in this case option two is the sensible one, but if sales had been eighty-five instead of ninety-five the opposite would have been true. In general, the more specialized the product and the greater the buoyancy in world markets, the greater the increase in the dollar price the UK firm may be able to extract without causing a major loss of orders.

The firm's decision will also be affected by cost considerations. If, for example, the firm is operating under economies of scale (i.e. unit costs fall as output expands) the reduction in output caused by raising US prices will increase unit costs and reduce profit. The pricing decision described above is depicted in Figure 5.2. Demand curve D_1 shows sales in the USA for a variety of UK sterling prices at an exchange rate of 1.75. There is an associated marginal revenue curve, MR, and a marginal cost curve, MC. The firm maximizes profit by selling Q_0 at price P_0. If the exchange rate rises to 1.95, sales fall at any previous sterling price so we have new demand and MR curves, D_2

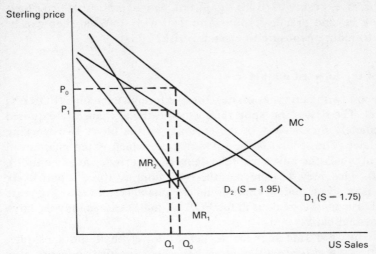

Figure 5.2 Effect of an appreciation in the $/£ exchange rate on a
UK firm with a heterogeneous product

and MR_2. The profit-maximizing sterling price, which the firm may
not know, is now P_1 and the output is Q_1.[2]

It should perhaps be pointed out, however, that in practice there
may be no reaction to an exchange-rate change in the short run.
Changing prices is costly and will have ramifications on dealers,
agents, output, employment and 'goodwill' so firms may wait and see
whether exchange-rate changes are permanent or transitory before
deciding on any actions. What a firm eventually does in response to
changes in exchange rates may also depend upon its circumstances.
Thus, if a UK firm has recently suffered a severe profits squeeze in
either its home or overseas market it may (assuming inelastic demand)
respond to an appreciation of sterling by raising dollar prices considerably. Conversely, a firm with a strong profits position could use the
opportunity of a depreciation in exchange rates to look for overseas
volume turnover by keeping prices and profit margins low. It may be
particularly interested in this sort of policy if stocks of unsold
'finished' goods are high.

5.3   REDUCING EXPOSURE TO RISK

It is clear that firms selling heterogeneous products are in a much
better position than those selling homogeneous ones in terms of
pricing strategies in response to exchange risk. Even so, for most

producers, exposure to risk is significant, which means that firms have to look beyond pricing responses to deal with it. What then can be done to reduce exposure to exchange risk?

Use of the forward market

There are two main types of 'deal' on the foreign exchange (FOREX) market. The first is the 'spot' rate, which is the exchange rate quoted immediately for delivery of the currency to the buyer two working days later. The second is the forward rate, which is the guaranteed price at which the buyer will take delivery of currency at some future period. This may be one month, two months, three months, six months or a year and, in exceptional circumstances, three to five years ahead. The market-makers in the FOREX market are mainly the large commercial banks.

The forward rate may be higher or lower than the spot rate, reflecting interest-rate differentials between respective countries over the length of the contract.[3] If interest rates in the USA, for example, were 2 per cent higher than in the UK the forward exchange rate ($/£) for sterling would have to be approximately 2 per cent higher than the spot rate. To see why, assume an importer has agreed to take delivery of a component from the USA in three months' time at a cost of $1,000. Assume three-month interest rates are 2 per cent in the UK and 4 per cent in the USA. Option 1 for our importer is to send a sum of money to the USA now and deposit it in a US bank to be worth $1,000 in three months. At 4 per cent interest, the relevant sum to invest in the USA would be $961.54 (as 961.54 × 1.04 = 1,000) and this requires paying £549.45 at a spot exchange rate of 1.75$/£. Alternatively, he could invest a sum of money in the UK at 2 per cent and then convert all this sterling into dollars in three months' time but at an agreed forward exchange rate 'today'. At UK interest rates of 2 per cent, £549.45 would be worth £560.4 in three months' time. For this to be a viable alternative, the forward rate would have to be 1,000/560.4 = 1.784$/£. That is, the forward rate for sterling must be approximately 2 per cent above the spot rate. The forward rate, therefore, is the one that maintains equilibrium in the market, for, in this case, if the forward rate were less than 2 per cent above the spot rate, all importers would take option 1. Option 1 involves purchasing spot dollars and selling spot sterling and this will put downward pressure on the $/£ exchange rate. Thus, with an unchanged forward rate, the spot–forward differential widens until the forward rate is 2 per cent above the spot rate. This process is known as covered (interest) arbitage.

A more precise definition of the relationship between spot and forward rates can be derived mathematically. Assume that a UK corporate treasurer has a sum of money, £X, which he can invest in the UK or the USA for one year, at which time the returns must be paid to his firm's UK shareholders. For the treasurer to be indifferent as to where the money is invested it has to be the case that returns in the UK from investing in the UK = the returns in the UK from investing in the USA.

The return from investing in the UK will be $X(1+r)$ where r is the UK rate of interest. The return in the UK from investing in the USA can be precisely evaluated by use of the spot exchange rate, $S(\$/£)$, and the forward exchange rate, $F(\$/£)$, for one year ahead. Converting the X pounds into dollars will give us XS dollars which will increase to $XS(1+r^*)$ dollars in one year's time if r^* is the US rate of interest. Dividing through by the forward rate, F converts the dollars into their sterling equivalent. Thus in equilibrium:

$$X (1 + r) = XS (1 + r^*)/F$$

which becomes:

$$\frac{S}{F} = \frac{1 + r}{1 + r^*}$$

or:

$$f - s = r^* - r \tag{5.1}$$

where $f = \ln (F)$ and $s = \ln (S)$ and we have used the approximation $\ln (1 + r^*) = r^*$, etc.[4].

Equation 5.1 is the so-called 'covered-interest parity' condition and in equilibrium it must apply to the FOREX market in general. If not, the demand for, say, sterling would not equal supply and the spot rate would change now. FOREX dealers will, therefore, quote a forward rate that is equal to $s + r^* - r$. The use of the forward rate eliminates risk from future exchange-rate changes as the rate is agreed today (even though the transaction takes place in three months' time). This does not, of course, mean that our corporate treasurer will necessarily use the forward market. One reason is that, in addition to the above quotation, he will also pay a commission to the FOREX dealer. More important, however, is that the firm has the option to take on 'open' or risky positions if it so chooses.

It must generally be the case, for equilibrium to hold in the FOREX market, that the expected return to investing in a foreign asset should be equal to that when investing in the domestic asset. Given the reasoning outlined in the 'certain' case above, this will be where, for the average investor, known returns from investing in the domestic country = the expected sterling return from investing in the foreign one. That is:

$$X (1 + r) = \frac{XS_t(1 + r^*)}{S_{e_{(t + 1)}}}$$

where X, r and r^* are as above, S_t = the spot exchange rate 'today' and S_e $(_{t+1})$ = the expected spot exchange rate one year from now.

This becomes as before:

$$\frac{S}{S_{e_{(t + 1)}}} = \frac{1 + r}{1 + r^*}$$

or:

$$S_{e_{(t + 1)}} - S_t = r^* - r \qquad (5.2)$$

This is known as the 'uncovered interest-rate parity condition'. Clearly, in equilibrium:

$$F = S_{e_{(t + 1)}} \qquad (5.3)$$

The individual firm is not, of course, bound by the expectations of the market. If the corporate treasurer of the firm thinks that, for example, the dollar will appreciate in excess of interest-rate differentials, i.e.:

$$(S_{e_{(t + 1)}} - S) > (r^* - r) \qquad (5.4)$$

he will be more likely to invest in the USA. Quite simply, he will now expect the money that he earns there to convert into more pounds in the future. Similarly, a UK businessman expecting to be paid for an export order to the USA in three months' time with the price already fixed in dollars will be likely to take an open position if he expects (5.4) to apply.

Most of the time, however, firms will be likely to use the forward market. The reason is that it completely avoids exchange risk to the importer or exporter. The importer knows the price he will have to pay and the exporter what he will receive. It will, therefore, be attractive to risk-averse firms. How mush use a particular firm will make of the forward market will, in any event, also depend upon the time interval between receipts and payments, and the countries in which it does business. The forward markets are most useful for short-term transactions in the world's major currencies.

Use of option contracts

Option contracts are forward contracts in which the customer has the option to invoke the contract either at any date from that of the contract being made to a specified future date or between any two specified dates in the future. For example, they are useful for situations when a business is not sure of the exact date on which it will want to buy or sell currency, and they avoid the necessity of having to extend forward contracts (which can be expensive on a short-term basis). The benefit to the firm is that foreign-exchange risk can be covered with certainty even when there is uncertainty about the precise date of the transaction. There is, however, a cost to the firm as it has to pay a premium in order to 'buy' the option contract from the dealer. If the firm's foreign currency receipts arrive on the expected date, the corporate treasurer undertakes only the forward-market transaction and he does not 'exercise' (i.e. 'cash in' his right to) the option. However, if the receipts arrive a little later than anticipated, he can exercise his option to purchase the currency at the pre-arranged fixed price (known as the strike price).

Hedging

In certain circumstances, it is impossible to use the forward market to minimize exposure to risk. Where, for example, there is no forward market for funds, say for five years ahead, a corporate treasurer can effectively hedge by using the foreign securities market (i.e. loan and asset purchases). For example, suppose a UK firm is to receive $10,000 in five years' time. If $r* = 0.1$, the annual rate of interest on a US bank loan, then a loan of $\$10,000/(1 + r*)^5 = \$6,209.2$ will accumulate debt interest of exactly $\$(10,000-6,209.2)$ over five years. The UK firm's $10,000 receipt in five years' time will pay off the principal and interest on a dollar loan of $6,209.2. But the $6,209.2 received today can be immediately switched into sterling in the spot market. Hence, although the $10,000 accrues in five years' time, the UK firm knows exactly how much sterling it represents today. The possibility clearly exists, then, of reducing exchange-rate risk by borrowing in the foreign currency against known future receipts in the foreign currency.

Risk spreading

It is generally accepted that it is not a good idea to put all your eggs into one basket, and this prompts the question as to whether our corporate treasurer could reduce his exposure to exchange risk for any given expected return by taking an open position in a number of currencies. To start the ball rolling, consider a highly simplified case where our UK treasurer transfers £10,000 into a yen current account earning zero interest and he expects the pound/yen rate to remain constant. His expected return is £10,000. If, however, there is a 50 per cent change in the value of the yen against sterling, the sterling value of his overseas asset changes by £5,000, a high degree of variability. As an alternative investment strategy, consider holding £5,000 each in yen and dollars where again we assume the investor expects zero change in the two bilateral rates against sterling. His expected return is again £10,000. Suppose, however, that he has observed that in the past, whenever the yen appreciates, the dollar always depreciates against sterling by an equal percentage amount (i.e. the correlation coefficient R between the two currencies equals -1). If this condition prevails in the future, it turns out that the variability in his sterling return is zero: i.e. whatever he gains on his yen assets he loses on his dollar assets. In fact, even if the two currencies tend to move in the same direction (but are not perfectly positively correlated), in this two-asset case there is still some reduction in the overall risk if the portfolio is diversified into the two currencies. It therefore appears that, if our fund manager can invest in a basket of currencies, particularly with some that have negative correlation (covariances), he will minimize the riskiness attached to the sterling value of his total assets. The optimum allocation between currencies to obtain the 'preferred' risk–return combination when there are more than two assets is a little complex, but for interested readers the methodology can be gleaned from the simple model given in the appendix. As one might expect, it depends on relative interest rates, the variability of each individual currency and the covariance of returns between currencies.

In practice, the overseas investment decision involves considerations other than simply exchange risk. The choice may involve a UK corporate treasurer investing in a 'dollar risky asset', for example, in a US government bond or equity. Here the dollar price of the asset is uncertain if sold on the open market before its maturity date. Formally this is easily handled in the framework outlined in the appendix, but in practice the number of 'balls being juggled' can lead to high information costs and a tendency to choose a subset of active assets for switching purposes.

The general strength of the foreign economy will influence sentiment in its equity market and hence price quotations on the stock exchange and may also affect its exchange rate in the same direction. This increases the potential variability in the sterling return. A mix of foreign equity and foreign government bonds (which are less influenced by the state of the economy) in a particular currency helps to minimize exposure to risk in this instance. Thus a corporate treasurer might engage in a sequential approach to portfolio management. He might, first, choose the optimum spread between currencies and second, diversify by type of asset in any one currency.

In the latter respect, liquidity will be an important consideration. The more liquid a financial asset, the more easily it may be switched into a means of payment without incurring high transactions costs (for example, brokerage and banking charges) or risk of capital loss because its market price is uncertain at the time of sale (for example, as with equities, government bonds). Cash and chequing accounts are highly liquid, as are overdraft facilities for large companies. Short-term assets such as 90-day certificates of deposit, Treasury bills and commercial bills are also highly liquid on the basis of this definition. Government bonds (gilt-edged stock), preference shares and equity involve higher transaction costs and greater risk of a capital loss (or gain) when sold and hence are deemed to be less liquid.

A multinational company may face an uncertain net inflow or outflow of funds on its profit and loss account and will need to act quickly to provide cash funds. In any one currency, firms will therefore hold a portfolio of assets throughout the liquidity spectrum. Then, an outflow of dollar payments, say, by a UK firm may be met by running down dollar chequing accounts, by increasing dollar over-drafts, or by selling short-term dollar assets (for example, US commercial bills) or long-term assets (for example, US government bonds) that are either near to maturity (and hence have a price close to their par or redemption value) or appear to command a favourable price in the market.

Investment in foreign subsidiaries

Although many considerations are involved in the costly business of setting up overseas subsidiaries, they do have a clear financial advantage in the avoidance of exchange risk. This is that production in a particular foreign country usually involves a close matching of receipts and disbursements in that particular foreign currency. Take, for example, the case of the European operations of Ford Motor Company. It produces and sells in a number of European countries, most of the currencies which are closely aligned in the European Monetary System (see Chapter 9). Ford can, therefore, borrow in, say, deutschmarks, pay German production workers in marks, and sell cars in Germany and throughout Europe with little exposure to exchange risk.

The main problem with setting up subsidiaries, in addition to the cost already referred to, is the remission of surplus profits to the parent company. The parent then has the problem, as outlined above, of the optimum allocation of funds between currencies. The Euro-currency markets (which include US dollars) provide a relatively cheap and quick way of switching funds between currencies and therefore subsidiaries, and hence holding a basket of Eurocurrencies minimizes exposure to exchange risk while maintaining a high degree of liquidity.

5.4   SUMMARY

Large multinationals, even those with a number of foreign subsidiaries, cannot avoid the problem of allocating some of their surplus funds in risky assets. They may be risky in terms of capital value, in terms of exchange risk and, where setting up subsidiaries or take-overs of foreign firms are involved, in terms of a whole host of production, marketing and managerial information costs. The decision to invest in foreign real assets may involve extensive market analysis of the foreign economy in general and also of particular markets (for example, for sales, labour, supplier companies), as well as of political risk. Ultimately, shareholders of the parent company will require dividend payments in the domestic currency and these will depend in part on movements in the bilateral rates between the domestic and the set of foreign currencies. Members of a corporate finance department will therefore need to trade off the liquidity, expected return and the various forms of risk, of which exchange risk is an important part, in deciding the optimal allocation of funds across assets in different currencies.

We have tried to develop the basic framework for analysing these problems from the point of view of the individual businessman in either a small company or a large multinational. Actual investment decisions require relatively complex decision rules (as well as good hunches!), but broadly speaking they involve factors discussed in the simple cases above. We hope, therefore, that the reader is now aware of the issues to be tackled by the corporate strategy department and the small exporter alike in overseas pricing, sales, production and portfolio investment decisions. We now turn to the forecasting of exchange rates which, of course, is an important element in the decision process of the firm.

5.5   APPENDIX: PORTFOLIO DIVERSIFICATION

We wish to demonstrate in a simple fashion the gains to be made from holding a diversified portfolio of assets. For the most part we utilize the simple 'two (risky) asset' model, but first some preliminaries.

Suppose the expected return in sterling of investing in a DM asset is £x, and in a yen-dominated asset is £y. Suppose investors have noted that, in the past, 'variability' as measured by the variance of each of the two assets is σ_x^2 and σ_y^2. In addition, the correlation coefficient between past movements in the returns on the DM and yen assets is $R(-1 < R < 1)$. Mathematically it may be shown that:

$$R = \sigma_{xy} / \sigma_x \sigma_y \qquad \text{(i)}$$

where σ_{xy} is the covariance between the two returns. If $R = +1$ the two assets are perfectly positively (linearly) related and the asset returns always move in the same direction. For $R = -1$ the converse applies and for $R = 0$ the asset returns are not (linearly) related. As we see below, the riskiness of an investment decision depends crucially on the sign and size of R. If $R = -1$, risk may be completely eliminated by a suitable combination of both DM and yen assets. Even if R is positive (but less than $+1$), riskiness is reduced (although not to zero) by diversification.

The problem facing the investor is to choose the proportion of his funds to invest in each asset in order to minimize risk. Should he put all his eggs in one basket (either DM or yen) and incur the risk of either σ_x^2 or σ_y^2, or should he hold some of each currency and if so how much of each? We begin with an algebraic exposition, but then demonstrate the points made using a simple numerical example. If he chooses to hold a proportion, b, in DM assets and $(1-b)$ in yen assets then the variance (risk) on his total portfolio, $T=bx + (1-b)y$, is (using (i)):

$$
\begin{aligned}
\text{Var}(T) &= \text{var}(bx + (1 - b)y) \\
&= b^2\text{var}(x) + (1 - b)^2 \, \text{var}(y) + 2b(1 - b)\text{cov}(x, \, y) \\
&= b^2\sigma_x^2 + (1 - b)^2\sigma_y^2 + 2b(1 - b)(R\sigma_x\sigma_y)
\end{aligned}
\qquad \text{(ii)}
$$

Knowing σ_x^2, σ_y^2 and R, the individual has to choose that value of b to minimize total risk, var (T). Using calculus, for a minimum we have:

$$\frac{\partial \, [\text{Var}(T)]}{\partial b} = 2b\sigma_x^2 - 2(1 - b)\sigma_y^2 + 2(1 - 2b)R\sigma_x\sigma_y = 0 \qquad \text{(iii)}$$

Solving (iii) for b we have:

$$b = (\sigma_y^2 - R\sigma_x\sigma_y)/(\sigma_x^2 + \sigma_y^2 - 2R\sigma_x\sigma_y) \qquad \text{(iv)}$$

Note that from (ii) 'the total variance' will be smallest when $R = -1$ and the largest when $R = +1$.

For illustrative purposes, assume $\sigma_x^2 = (0.4)^2$, $\sigma_y^2 = (0.5)^2$, $R = 0.25$ (i.e. positive correlation). Then the value of b for minimum variance using (iv) is:

$$b = \frac{(0.5)^2 - 0.25(0.4)(0.5)}{(0.4)^2 + (0.5)^2 - 2(0.25)(0.4)(0.5)} = \frac{20}{31}$$

and substituting this value of b in (ii) we have:

$$\text{var}(T) = 12.1\%$$

which is smaller than the variance if all his wealth had been put in DM, $\sigma_x^2 = (0.4)^2 = 16\%$, or all in yen, $\sigma_y^2 = (0.5)^2 = 25\%$. If the correlation coefficient is $R = -1$, then using (iv) we obtain $b = 5/9$ and substituting this value in (ii) we obtain var $(T) = 0$. Thus all risk can be diversified when the two asset returns are perfectly negatively correlated. It follows from this analysis that an individual asset may be highly risky (i.e. high variance), but if it has a negative covariance with assets already held in the portfolio it will be highly sought after (and command a high price) as it will tend to reduce overall portfolio risk.

Other considerations

Calculation of the minimum risk portfolio requires a computer analysis as the number of covariance terms σ_{ij} increases rapidly as more assets are added. Also, in practice, an investor will be faced with a somewhat more complex algebraic problem than that analysed above as he will wish to maximize some relationship that involves both expected return and risk: he will accept more risk only if there is a higher expected return (Cuthbertson 1986). Formal mathematical models (for example, expected utility maximization) are able to deal with such problems, but we cannot deal with these here (see, for example, Davis and Pointon 1984, Allen 1983) and in general it is found that individuals do not have to invest in a very wide range of assets to reduce diversifiable risk. About twenty is probably sufficient.

Note that the above analysis can also be applied (in principle at least) to decisions about direct investment (for example, in subsidiary companies) in a number of foreign countries. The riskiness of each (real) investment project in terms of expected profits provides the σ_is and the covariance between currency movements will be a major determinant of the covariances (correlation) between the different projects, σ_{ij}. In principle the optimal proportions, b, of direct invest-ment funds in each country can then be determined in the manner described above.

Finally, it is worth emphasizing that the above formal analysis neglects issues such as alternative managerial goals (for example, empire building), considerations of liquidity, risk of bankruptcy, etc., that occur in 'real world' decisions.

NOTES

1 The exchange rate, S, here is quoted in 'indirect' terms of $/£. An increase in S in this case means an appreciation of the pound and a depreciation of the dollar. The opposite would apply if S were quoted in 'direct' terms of £/$. Conventions differ on this. In the UK, the indirect quote is used whereas in the USA, for example, the direct quote is adopted.

2 The pivoting of the new demand and MR curves can be explained by the use of simple calculus.
Assume a linear demand curve:

$$Q = a - \frac{bP_{£}S}{P^*}$$

then:

$$\frac{P_{£}S}{P^*} = \frac{Q - a}{-b}$$

and:

$$P_{£} = \frac{(Q - a)\{P^*\}}{-bS}$$

$$\frac{dP£}{dQ} = \frac{-P^*}{Sb}$$

This is the slope of the demand curve. The higher S is, the smaller is the slope that pivots from point a on the Q axis. The slope of the MR curve is twice the slope of the demand curve.

3 Forward rates are quoted as a premium or discount on spot rates. If the dollar, for example, is at a premium three months forward of 0.32 cents and the spot rate is 1.5284 ($/£), then the three months forward rate is 1.5252 ($/£).

4 As by the rules of logarithms:

$$\ln (F/S) = \ln (F) - \ln (S) = f - s$$
$$\text{where } f = \ln (F), \, s = \ln (S)$$

Similarly:

$$\ln \frac{[(1 + r)]}{[1 + r^*]} = \ln (1 + r) - \ln (1 + r^*) \simeq r - r^*$$

where '$\simeq$' means 'approximately equal to' and we have used:

$$[\ln (1 + r) \simeq r \text{ for } r < 1 \text{ (for example, } r = 0.02 \text{ or } 2\%)]$$

6 The international environment 2
The determination of exchange rates

Exchange rates are very difficult to forecast and this is, of course, why it is sensible for businessmen to adopt strategies such as use of the forward market, hedging and maintaining a portfolio of foreign assets. Even so, in deciding what to do in particular circumstances, it is probably important to form an expectation of future exchange-rate movements. This can be done in a variety of ways. The least sophisticated involve graphical and other simple statistical methods, while the most sophisticated use complete macroeconomic models. We now examine the options in detail.

6.1 GRAPHICAL METHODS

The use of graphical methods is usually referred to as chartism as those employing these methods use charts to plot exchange-rate movements. Here a time series graph of the exchange rate is projected into the future, as shown in Figure 6.1

A relatively more sophisticated method of picking out turning points on the 'chart' is to look at successive values of the change in the exchange rate, (s_t-s_{t-1}). As an upper turning point is approached (for example, B in Figure 6.1), then (s_t-s_{t-1}) gets smaller and is zero at the peak, before becoming negative. Thus a decreasing value in successive periods for (s_t-s_{t-1}) might signify an imminent turning point. However, chartism, even sophisticated chartism, is hazardous. For example, suppose the exchange-rate path goes through a small 'step up' (for example, E-F-G, Figure 6.1). Here (s_t-s_{t-1}) approaches zero in successive time periods but s continues to rise in subsequent periods (to point H).

Clearly, looking at charts seems very simple. In practice, however, chartist projections may be based on considerably more complex analysis, with computer programs used to give the forecast plots. Computers can also be programmed to give buy and sell prompts to

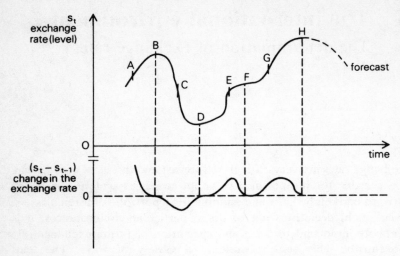

Figure 6.1 Forecasting the exchange rate by chartism methods

FOREX dealers in certain circumstances. Suppose, for example, the
\$/£ exchange rate over the past year had fluctuated consistently
between 1.95 and 1.75. This would suggest that each time the rate
dropped to 1.75 speculators or Central Banks considered the pound to
be undervalued and bought pounds. Similarly, every time the pound
approached 1.95 it was generally regarded as overvalued and pounds
were sold. In this way 1.95 and 1.75 may be considered resistance
points.

If, subsequently, the exchange rate fell below 1.75, this would
suggest that the perception of the value of the pound had changed. The
chartist would now suspect that the exchange rate had broken out
from the resistance level and might be expected to continue to fall until
a new resistance level had been reached.

A difficulty with all this is that, as many chartists work on similar
lines, their predictions can be self-fulfilling. There may, therefore, be
dramatic falls in the value of the currency once a resistance level has
been breached. As we shall see below, there are other reasons why this
can occur. Despite the crudeness of the chartist approach, it is
extensively used both for exchange rates and share prices by a number
of City forecasting firms, sometimes with a reasonable degree of
success (Buckley 1986).

6.2 SIMPLE STATISTICAL MODELS

The following simple statistical models have often been advocated for use by business forecasters:

$$s_t = s_{t-1} \qquad \text{random walk} \qquad (6.1)$$

$$s_t = f_{t-1} \qquad \text{forward rate} \qquad (6.2)$$

$$s_t = a_1 s_{t-1} + a_2 s_{t-2} + a_3 s_{t-3} \quad \text{autoregressive} \qquad (6.3)$$

The random walk model, (6.1), assumes that the exchange rate today is the best indicator for the next period. Alternatively, the forward rate model, (6.2) assumes that today's forward rate is the best predictor of the next period's spot rate. Finally, the autoregressive model, (6.3), assumes that the next period's spot rate is a weighted average of past spot rates. The weights, a_i, can be obtained by regression analysis.

Interestingly, there is some evidence (Meese and Rogoff 1983) that these simple models perform well in relation to the more complex single equation models below. Overall, their results were relatively unfavourable to the econometric equations and frequently the 'best' forecasting equation was a no-change random walk model.

It also seems to be the case that professional commercial forecasters do not appear to yield, on average, better forecasts of the spot rate over one to twelve months than one would obtain using the forward rate, although individual organizations can do relatively well.

6.3 ECONOMIC FORECASTING MODELS

These are based upon the view that exchange rates are ultimately dependent upon economic fundamentals. Under floating exchange rates, and with no Central Bank intervention in the FOREX market, the demand for foreign currency must equal the supply on to the FOREX market if FOREX dealers are to hold spot exchange rates at current values. For this to be the case it has to be true of the balance of payments that:

$$\text{current account} + \text{capital account} = 0$$

Changes in the underlying determinants of either of these accounts will cause changes in the demand and supply of home country currency. If supply exceeds demand for the pound, for example, the pound will be marked down. What then are the underlying determinants?

a) Relative goods prices

The notion here is of purchasing power parity, or PPP, and is that an item that costs £1 in London should cost $1.75 in New York if the exchange rate is $1.75 to the £1. In general:

$$P* = PS \qquad (6.4)$$

where P = price in the UK of a basket of goods; $P*$ = price in the USA of the same basketful; and S = the relevant exchange rate in terms of dollars per pounds.

However, the exchange rate, in practice, must reflect more than just the relative price of goods in, say, London and New York. For how else can the fluctuation in the 1980s in the $/£ exchange rate from 2.40 to just over 1 be explained? Clearly, there were times when British goods were relatively cheap and relatively expensive to US customers. (Relative goods prices are obviously a measure of 'price competitiveness' and the latter is often referred to in textbooks as the real exchange rate.)

b) The level of domestic demand

The higher this is, the higher the level of imports and the lower the exchange rate.

c) The level of world demand

The precise impact of a rise in this on a country's exchange rate will depend upon which goods are being increasingly demanded and which countries are producing them.

d) Relative interest rates

These affect capital flows and *ceteris paribus* it would be expected that, if UK nominal interest rates were *suddenly* increased relative to those elsewhere, money would tend to flow into the UK and the pound would immediately appreciate. This is the relationship suggested by the interest term in 6.6 below and by the overshooting model (see below in section on 'complete models').

In reality, *ceteris paribus* conditions will not apply and *persistently* high domestic interest rates may be associated with other factors (e.g. high level of domestic inflation) which cause or are expected to cause the domestic exchange rate to depreciate in the long run. Thus an *unanticipated* increase in UK interest rates is likely to lead to an appreciation of the pound while a *persistently high* UK interest rate may be associated with a depreciating pound (as in Figure 6.2 below). The net effect of these changes in interest rates, therefore, depends on whether the rise in interest rates is 'unexpected' or has persisted for some time. In 6.6 below we assume an 'unexpected' or sudden policy change which raises domestic interest rates so that the effect is to lead to an immediate appreciation of sterling.

Uncovered interest-rate parity can throw some light on these matters. This (as outlined in Chapter 5) implies that, in equilibrium, the expected appreciation in a foreign currency is just equal to the interest differential in favour of the domestic currency. That is:

$$(s^e_{t+1} - s_t) = (r^* - r) \qquad (6.5)$$

If this condition does not hold there is clearly an advantage in switching between currencies. If for example, the dollar is expected to appreciate against the pound by 2 per cent over the next three months, but UK (three-month) interest rates are just 1 per cent higher than American ones, it would pay to change pounds into dollars now and invest in the USA. This would continue until, for example, UK interest rates rose sufficiently to stop the outflow of funds. The UIP condition is incorporated in the complete models of the exchange rate outlined below.

Single equation econometric models

Factors a to d provide the basis for a number of exchange-rate forecasting models used in the UK in the 1970s. Such models are represented by equations of the following type:

$$
\overset{-}{} \qquad \overset{+}{} \qquad \overset{-}{}
$$
$$S = f\{(p - p^*),\ CB,\ (r - r^*)\} \qquad (6.6)$$

where the signs are as indicated for S measured in dollars per pounds; P refers to price levels; and CB = current-account balance. Normally CB and $r-r^*$ would be considered as short-term influences on S with relative prices affecting the exchange rate in the long term. There are some variations to this model. The above is a Keynesian version (e.g. the NIESR model), but a monetarist one would substitute money-supply figures for relative prices. The model can be estimated by linear regression. One problem with it is that it requires the business forecaster to input his own guesses for the RHS variables in (6.6). Moreover, no account is taken of the feedback effects of changes in the exchange rate on these RHS variables. Take, for example, an increase in the money supply. This would be expected to lead to an increase in (p–p*) and to a depreciation of the exchange rate. But this depreciation will, in turn, raise import prices and hence the domestic price level, p, and any change in the current-account deficit will be reflected in changes in CB. A final problem is that no account is taken of the role of expectations. These are probably crucial in explaining why exchange-rate movements very often do not relate to economic fundamentals. This suggests that a more sophisticated approach is required.

Complete models

In such models the exchange rate is part of a simultaneous equation system modelling the whole economy. Key assumptions are usually that goods prices are 'sticky' (i.e. fixed) in the short run, that capital flows are covered by uncovered interest-rate parity, UIP, and that expectations about the exchange rate play an important role in determining current movements in the spot exchange rate.

Consider, for example, the case of a reduction in the money supply and assume that FOREX dealers operate on the principle of purchasing power parity, PPP. If so, they will now work out that the fall in the money supply should mean a fall in the price level and, given equation (6.4), an appreciation of the exchange rate. If they think the pound is going to appreciate they will buy pounds now and it will therefore appreciate. If prices are 'sticky' they will remain high for a while, and, given the new lower money supply, this implies a relative shortage of money. Interest rates will now rise and induce more money to flow across the exchanges, leading to a further appreciation of the currency in question. In other words, it will at least for a time overshoot its long-term level. The position is illustrated in Figure 6.2

Assume that the UK economy is in equilibrium at the time, t, when the UK government reduces the money supply. Instead of settling at a new equilibrium at point B immediately, the exchange rate moves to level C before gradually depreciating to D at time t. Such overshooting does seem consistent with the facts. Note, for example, the fluctuations in the value of the dollar referred to above.

The above scenario emphasizes the complexity involved in forecasting the exchange rate. Day-to-day and month-to-month changes in exchange rates are clearly more volatile than movements in economic fundamentals would suggest. Expectations are clearly important and so may be the irrational activities of chartists and other market players. Moreover, the impact of overshooting may well be long term

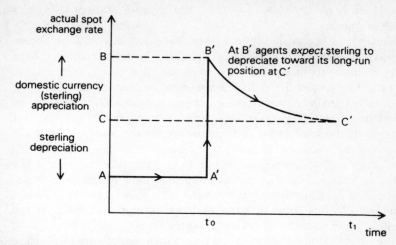

Figure 6.2 Exchange rate overshooting

and in some cases irreversible. A rising exchange rate, as in the above case, leads to reduced price competitiveness in international markets and to a consequent loss of export markets and to import penetration. The appreciation of sterling in the period 1979–81, for example, contributed to the rapid fall of about 15 per cent in manufacturing output over the period and to the subsequent reverse multiplier effects that led to a fall in total output of some 2–3 per cent over two years.

Are there some self-correcting mechanisms that can reverse the above decline in output, consequent on the overshooting in the exchange rate? The answer is yes, but these appear to work slowly and it may be the case that output does not fully attain its previous level. This would be a Keynesian viewpoint rather than a monetarist one. As domestic demand falls in the recession, this leads to increased unemployment and downward pressure on wages and hence on prices (see Chapter 8 for further details). In addition, lower domestic import prices, consequent on the appreciation, feed directly into business costs and lower prices. As domestic prices fall, this offsets the adverse competitiveness effects of the nominal appreciation and net trade volume (i.e. exports less imports) begins to expand and output rises. As prices fall (or rise less fast), holders of financial assets who have interest rates that are sticky or zero (for example, current accounts, some bank and building society deposits) feel 'richer': the value of their assets rises, in terms of their purchasing power over goods. This appears to have a powerful positive impact on consumer spending

(Davidson *et al.* 1978, Hendry and von Ungern-Sternberg 1979) and hence output.

However, a Keynesian-type supply-side effect has adverse consequences, working via the productivity of the labour force. Older workers made redundant in the manufacturing sector may be unable or unwilling to retrain in the new expanding sectors (for example, insurance, banking, computers), while young potential entrants to the labour force may be permanently deterred from seeking employment because of the frustration in their unsuccessful search for what are perceived by them to be acceptable job offers. Hence the overall productivity of the potential labour force may fall and with it the economy's overall level of potential output. Thus the adverse consequences of overshooting on real output may be permanent, although there are obvious gains in terms of lower inflation working via the Phillips curve and import prices (Chapter 8).

The above points emphasize the need for exchange-rate forecasting based upon complete macroeconomic models and for expectations to be explicitly included within them. How the latter can be done is illustrated by a version of the Treasury model (HM Treasury 1982). In this version, the expected change in the exchange rate depends upon the change in its long-run value and its current deviation from its long-run level $(s_t - \bar{s}_t)$. The long-run rate, $\bar{s}_t$, is assumed to be influenced primarily by a weighted average of domestic costs (broadly Keynesian view) and relative (i.e. foreign to domestic) monetary growth (i.e. broadly monetarist view). The spot rate may then be determined by an equation like (6.6), but with the expected change in the exchange rate included as an additional independent variable to capture speculative capital flows (HM Treasury model 1982). Note that the expectations scheme for the spot rate in the Treasury is arbitrary and does not coincide with the predictions of the spot rate obtained using the forecasts of the complete Treasury model; agents are assumed to make systematic errors.

Unfortunately, even complete macroeconometric models are not accurate predictors of exchange rates, particularly in the short run. An explanation can be found in the impact of information or 'news' on exchange-rate changes.

Up to this point we have confined our analysis to a discussion of the 'fundamental' variables that are thought to influence exchange rates (for example, relative prices, current balance, interest rates). However, day-to-day and month-to-month changes in spot rates appear to be more volatile than would be predicted using equations involving changes in these fundamental variables. Does this imply that FOREX dealers create short-term instability of exchange rates? A useful starting point in examining this question is to consider the UIP relationship:

$$(s^e_{t+1} - s_t) = (r^* - r)_t \qquad (6.7)$$

Suppose FOREX dealers are 'rational' and hence correctly guess on average the actual future spot rate, s_{t+1}. Then we must have $s_{t+1} = s^e_{t+1} + u_{t+1}$ where u_{t+1} is a random forecast error (i.e. $s_{t+1} - s^e_{t+1} = u_{t+1}$) with a zero mean value. It follows that:

$$s_{t+1} - s_t = (r^* - r)_t + u_{t+1} \qquad (6.8)$$

Thus the actual change in the spot rate, $(s_{t+1} - s_t)$, equals the interest differential plus a forecast error. It is the latter which, although zero on average, may take large positive or negative values in any single period and 'cause' volatility in exchange-rate movements. For example, suppose there is an unexpected increase in the foreign interest rate, between t and t + 1. The actual spot rate of the domestic currency would then depreciate below the level expected before this new information (or 'news') became available and u_{t+1} would take a positive value. Such 'jumps' take place instantaneously as FOREX dealers alter their quoted spot price over the telephone. In contrast, consider an announced increase in the United States (foreign) interest rate to become effective in one month's time or, more realistically, a guess by FOREX dealers that the policy of the Federal Reserve Board will be to reduce monetary growth in one month's time. In both cases FOREX dealers react immediately and mark sterling down, as agents attempt to get rid of sterling assets today. When the US interest rate alters in one month's time, the spot rate will remain unchanged as the anticipated event will already have been incorporated in their view of the appropriate exchange rate. This highlights the different response of the exchange rate to anticipated and unanticipated events.

The exchange rate may 'jump' before the actual causal event takes place if the latter is anticipated, while unanticipated events may lead to major revisions in expectations and volatile jumps in the exchange rate from week to week. Although such volatility affects the usefulness of macroeconomic forecasting models in the short run they may, of course, be of some use for long-run planning. For company treasurers, the existence of this short-run volatility should not be a serious problem as far as most currencies are concerned, since as argued in Chapter 5, various strategies can be adopted to deal with it.

6.4 SUMMARY: FUNDAMENTALS AND THE EXCHANGE RATE

Exchange rates are so difficult to forecast that businessmen must hedge against exchange risk whenever possible and choose a portfolio of foreign assets to reduce risk to an acceptable level while earning a sufficient return and maintaining adequate liquidity in foreign assets.

The exchange rate impinges on the cost and production decisions of firms, as changes in the real exchange rate can have powerful effects on price competitiveness and sales volume both abroad and in the home market. Exchange rate overshooting is far from a theoretical curiosity. Exchange-rate forecasting may be hazardous, whatever method is used, and pehaps the major useful practical element that emerges is the possibility of assessing alternative scenarios using a complete macro model, in which the behaviour of the exchange rate is usually of crucial importance. Some ideas of the sensitivity of business decisions on pricing, output and asset diversification to changes in the exchange rate and other exogenous variables (for example, world demand) can then be ascertained and used in the firm's planning process. The degree of uncertainty can then be crudely quantified and assessed and, if nothing else, the businessman can hold a coherent view of future exchange-rate movements given his assumptions about the future course of government policy and external events. These issues are discussed further in Chapter 9.

7 The financial environment

In the previous two chapters we discussed the factors influencing the allocation of funds between various foreign assets. In this chapter we concentrate on the determination of domestic interest rates, although clearly the interdependence between domestic and foreign financial markets cannot be ignored.

Movements in interest rates have a direct and important impact upon the firm. First and most obvious, actual changes and expected future movements in interest rates influence a firm's *real* investment decisions. This applies to longer-term projects such as expansion of existing plant, the purchase of new machinery or a new vehicle fleet as well as short-term investment, for example, in deciding what quantity of stocks of raw materials or finished goods to hold.

Interest rates may influence both the amount of real investment and its timing. In determining the former we noted in Chapter 3 the use of the net present value technique, which requires knowledge of the cost of funds (cost of borrowing). The lower is the cost of funds, the higher, *ceteris paribus*, is the level of investment. On the question of the timing of investment, if the businessman believes that interest rates will fall in the near future it will be advantageous for the firm to postpone its purchase of capial equipment in order to obtain more favourable terms.

In principle, real investment should respond to changes in real interest rates, that is, the nominal (percentage) interest rate, r, less the expected rate of price inflation. If inflation is expected to be 10 per cent p.a. over the life of the investment project and the cost of borrowing is r = 12 per cent p.a. then the investment project should be just as profitable as when r = 3 per cent p.a. and inflation is 1 per cent p.a. because the real interest is 2 per cent in both cases. This result is incorporated in the NPV formula for investment since, if nominal profits (returns) provide the numerator, then the nominal interest rate is used to discount future receipts (in the denominator), thus cancelling out the effect of inflation on the NPV of the project. However, because nominal interest rates can move independently of inflation, a change in the former often implies a change in real interest rates and hence in the NPV of the project and of the investment decision.

Second, changes in interest rates may influence the liquidity and hence potential solvency of firms. If a firm has a high level of income gearing (i.e. net interest payments on short-term liabilities as a proportion of revenue or profits), then a rise in interest rates will increase interest payments, and if a cushion of liquid assets is not readily available the firm may experience cash flow problems and may possibly have to go into liquidation.

Third, when a firm undertakes a large investment project, such as building a new UK plant, then the mix of finance will be partly influenced by the relative interest cost of various forms of finance. For example, what proportion of funds should come from retained profits, bank advances, issues of commercial bills, debenture or equity? This decision depends upon the businessman's view of current interest rates and share price trends. Even if a firm uses retained profits as a source of finance the cost of such funds is not zero, but the interest the firm could make by investing the funds elsewhere (e.g. in a deposit account). Because of the low transactions costs of bank lending (which is now available on a longer-term basis of up to twenty years as well as short-term overdrafts) and issuing commercial bills, these 'outside' sources of finance are used more frequently than 'costly' debenture and equity issues. It is perhaps also worth noting that some firms expand by take-overs. They borrow funds in order to purchase the shares of other firms whose shares they believe are undervalued, given the value of the real capital equipment and goodwill of the firm under threat of take-over. However, this is not an expansion in aggregate investment in the economy, but merely a change in ownership and control. (The latter may lead to higher aggregate investment in the future.) It could be argued that a lower general level of interest rates encourages borrowing for such take-over bids (for example, Guinness for Distillers in the United Kingdom in 1986).

In the USA in the 1980s a number of take-over bids were financed by issuing fixed-interest bonds to investors ('junk bonds'). The idea was that, after the take-over, the assets of the firm (e.g. plant, machinery, goodwill) could be quickly sold off (i.e. 'asset stripping') and the funds used to buy back some or all of the high-risk, high-interest bonds. However, for some time after the take-over, the purchasers of the firm would have to finance high interest payments on the junk bonds (i.e. such firms were highly geared) and the failure to do so resulted in numerous bankruptcy proceedings in the USA.

In this chapter, we concentrate on the proximate (immediate) determinants of interest rates as a result of changes emanating in the financial markets. (In Chapter 9 we discuss the wider impact of interest rates on the real economy.) In the next section, 7.1, we discuss the main sources (i.e. suppliers) of funds and the main users (i.e. borrowers). This flow of funds approach highlights the importance of financial intermediaries in channelling funds from surplus (i.e. in credit) to deficit (i.e. borrower) units. Financial intermediaries play a very active role in financial markets and hence, by collectively altering the supply and demand for various assets such as equities and gilt-edged stock, they directly influence relative interest rates (for example, the rate of interest on bank loans relative to the cost of debenture finance).

With the advent of the 'Big Bang' in the City of London in October 1986, the increased competitive element in financial markets has been substantially enhanced. Changes like the abolition of fixed commissions on buying and selling financial assets and permitting foreign financial institutions to operate on the United Kingdom stock exchange have tended to make interest rates and other asset prices more responsive to the market forces of supply and demand. A more competitive approach has also been independently adopted by building societies in the provision of housing finance (mortgages) and in competitive bidding for deposits and this has been reflected in the Building Societies Act in the United Kingdom, which allows societies to operate as diverse, flexible financial institutions rather akin to commercial banks. Banks in the United Kingdom have, since the introduction of the policy of competition and credit control (CCC) in 1971, been very market orientated in their provision of bank advances and in providing a wide variety of 'deposits' for their customers to invest in. In short, interest rates in bank and mortgage markets have now largely ceased to be set by a cartel of institutions and are now subject to market forces. In addition, increased liberalization appears to have led to a vast innovation in the provision of financial services, from cash dispenser machines to complex 'swap' arrangements between banks. All in all, we cannot begin to understand the determination of a wide range of interest rates until we investigate the main types of financial deals undertaken in the City of London and other international financial centres.

Having looked at the main financial agencies we turn to an examination of the processes of relative interest rate movements in 7.2.

We then turn in 7.3 to the influence of the government, working through the Central Bank, on financial markets. Here we analyse the relationship between monetary and fiscal policy and their impact on the absolute level of certain key interest rates. The latter comprise the short rate on 91-day Treasury bills or commercial bills and the long rate on gilt-edged stock. Changes in these two key rates feed through the whole of the financial system and lead to changes in many other interest rates and indeed in some relative interest rates. Some of these effects operate via the yield curve. Thus, if the Central Bank operates on short rates it may be able to have a (fairly) direct impact on long rates. The latter then influence equity prices and hence the real investment decisions of firms. The impact of foreign interest rates and perceptions of risk factors on domestic interest rates are also discussed. We then look at interest rate forecasts in 7.4 and end the chapter with a brief summary.

7.1   THE FLOW OF FUNDS

The flow of funds refers to the exchange of assets (and debts) between various sectors of the economy, a stylized version of which is shown in Table 7.1. (For an actual flow of funds matrix, see Table 1.1 of *Financial Statistics* or the *Bank of England Quarterly Bulletin*.)

The main surplus unit with funds to on-lend is the personal sector, which invariably has positive nominal saving (i.e. income less consumer spending and new housing investment). Simplifying somewhat, these surplus funds are borrowed by the government and the non-financial company sector. Broadly speaking, the government has to borrow when tax receipts fall short of government expenditure, that is, when the authorities have a positive public sector borrowing requirement (PSBR). The company sector is a net borrower because its retained profits are usually insufficient to finance its real investment plans.

Of course, if a unit is in surplus that does not mean to say it has no outstanding debts, merely that its increase in assets outweighs the increase in its liabilities. For example, the personal sector, even though it is a surplus unit, may take out additional bank loans or house mortgages. Also within a particular sector, one group may lend to another as, for example, when one person's building society deposit is on-lent to another person taking out a new mortgage. It follows that a 'surplus unit' provides a net flow of funds to other deficit units.

The major portion of the funds from people to government and the company sector are channelled via financial intermediaries such as

Table 7.1 Stylized flow of funds (excluding overseas transactions)[7]

| Assets/liabilities | Personal sector | Industrial and commercial companies | Sector | | Public sector | Sum of rows[3] |
			Monetary sector[1]	Other financial institutions[2]		
1 Finance surplus[4]	2500	-700	700	100	-2600	0
Increase in assets (+) and liabilities (-)						
2 Cash	100	100	-200	0	0	0
3 Bank deposits	1000	1000	-2300	300	0	0
4 Building society deposits	2000	0	0	-2000	0	0
5 LAPF[5]	2000	0		-2000	0	0
6 Treasury bills	200	200	100	0	-500	0
7 Commercial bills	200	-1000	200	600	0	0
8 British government securities (gilt-edged stock)	800	200	0	1000	-2000	0
9 Company securities (equities)	300	400	0	-700	0	0
10 Bank advances	-1700	-1500	2700	500	0	0
11 Building society mortgages	-2000	0	0	2000	0	0
12 Sum of column	2900	-600	500	400	-2500	700
13 Balancing item[6]	-400	-100	200	-300	-100	0

Notes:
1 Banks and licensed deposit takers.
2 LAPF, building societies, etc.
3 Net claims are zero across any one asset/liability.
4 Broadly speaking, revenue less running costs less investment and stockbuilding.
5 LAPF are considered part of the personal sector.
6 Statistical discrepancies between 1 and 12, i.e. row 13 = row 1 – row 12.
7 For simplicity we ignore the overseas sector.

banks, building societies, life assurance and pension funds (LAPF), finance houses and unit trusts. Why, in the main, have financial intermediaries taken up this role in preference to direct lending from persons to our deficit units? The main reasons are transactions, search and information costs, and risk spreading. Specialist firms can more easily assess the creditworthiness of borrowers, and reap economies of scale in buying and selling financial assets (and property). By taking advantage of 'the law of large numbers' they can hold less low-yield precautionary balances and pass on this cost saving to borrowers or lenders. For example, the net daily flow of cash out of a large commercial bank is much less than the 'over-the-counter' gross flow because a large number of surplus and deficit cash units use the same branch on any one day. In contrast, a small operator would have to hold a high level of 'till money'.

Finally, as we noted in Chapter 5, if one has enough funds to invest in a wide range of 'risky' assets (each with a variable market price), then the 'risk' on the whole portfolio is much less than holding only a few assets. This tends to lead to specialization and the development of large financial intermediaries. This is not, of course, to deny that there are some relatively small direct transactions between surplus and deficit units, such as purchase by people of gilt-edged stock via the National Savings Stock Register, or share purchases on the stock exchange.

Although new surplus funds are channelled into various financial assets it must be remembered that there are vast quantities of existing assets traded on the market and these transactions naturally also have a major impact on interest rates and share prices.

We have identified the main surplus and deficit units and we now analyse the main assets and liabilities of each sector. Naturally, most institutions will hold a wide range of assets and liabilities of differing maturities and liquidity. All we can do here is highlight the key activities of the various sectors, which will enable us to determine the main source of possible changes in particular interest rates.

Members of the personal sector on-lend via building society deposits to other members of the personal sector in the form of new mortgages for house purchase. The building society itself will hold a small amount of precautionary liquid assets (for example, cash, bank deposits, short-term bills). Similarly, the personal sector holds a substantial number of bank deposits, some of which are on-lent to people and some to our deficit units in the form of bank loans to companies. A large proportion of a firm's investment finance outside of retained earnings comes from bank advances. The personal sector also holds a reasonable proportion of its financial wealth in stocks and shares.

The LAPF are key protagonists in financial markets. They take funds mainly from the personal sector in the form of life assurance policies and compulsory pension payments. As these are long-term liabilities from the point of view of the LAPF, a large proportion are invested in gilt-edged stock, equities (i.e. stocks and shares), real estate (property) and foreign assets. In this way they match the maturity date of future pension payments to the redemption date of their assets. However, they can and do rely on portfolio diversification to spread their risks, and also hold a relatively small cushion of liquid assets. The build-up of foreign financial assets (for example, shares of Ford US, US government long-term bonds) has proceeded apace after the abolition of the United Kingdom exchange controls in 1979. LAPF will actively trade with a proportion of their domestic and foreign portfolio and hence have an important influence on domestic interest rates. This is particularly true concerning their dealings with the government broker over the purchase and sale of government stock. In this way the authorities can seek to influence long rates of interest directly, an issue we take up below when discussing control of the money supply.

The banking system takes in deposits from the personal and company sectors and on-lends to the government by its purchase of new issues of Treasury bills and gilts, but the main part of its business consists of loans (i.e. bank advances and overdrafts) to people and companies. The banks have a special position in the financial system because their liabilities (i.e. current and deposit accounts) constitute the main part of the money supply, a variable the authorities often seek to control. In the United Kingdom system there are a unique set of institutions known as the discount houses which act as intermediaries between the banks and the Central Bank. Instead of the Bank of England directly buying and selling bills (i.e. short-term assets) from the banks, thus altering their cash balances or 'reserves', it usually does so in an indirect manner. The banks lend money to the discount houses (i.e. 'money at call') and the latter purchase bills from the Bank of England. Conversely, if the banks require cash they call in their 'call loans' from the discount houses, which then have to sell bills to obtain the finance required. Thus for analytic purposes we can consider the above as a direct sale (or purchase) of bills by the banks to the Central Bank. It is these dealings by the Bank of England in the bill market, which mainly relate to commercial bills, that allow the Bank to influence short-term interest rates and the money supply.

7.2   RELATIVE INTEREST RATES AND YIELDS

The question of interest here is how relative interest rates vary over time. In general, 'risky assets' are likely to have a higher yield than less risky assets. Also, the ease (i.e. low brokerage or transactions costs) with which assets can be turned into 'money' will determine their relative attractiveness. Thus, highly liquid assets such as chequing accounts tend to earn zero[1] or low interest, although with financial innovation and 'electronic banking' more chequing accounts now earn interest. Short-term marketable assets such as commercial bills issued by 'deficit' firms earn slightly more interest. Long-term marketable assets, such as gilts, generally (but not always) earn a higher return than short-term assets because of the risk element: their market price, if sold before the redemption date, is uncertain. Debentures and equity also have highly volatile market prices depending upon the actual and expected profitability of particular companies.

At this point, how one measures 'the return' on a particular asset needs some comment. Clearly, if you hold an asset to maturity (e.g. three-month 'bill') a sensible measure of the return is the interest rate or 'yield to maturity' expressed at an annual rate. Thus, if one purchases a pure discount bill (i.e. one that pays no coupon) with three months to maturity with a redemption value of £100, at a market price of £97, then the yield to maturity is $r = [(100–97)/97] \times (12/3) \times 100\% = 12.37$ per cent per annum. (Note that, by convention, the 'yield' uses the market price of 97 in the denominator.) This is commonly referred to as the interest rate on the bill.

Now consider a bond with two years to maturity with a purchase price of $P_B = £200$. For purely illustrative purposes, suppose this bond pays out £110 in the first year and £121 in the second year and that is all. (These known periodic payments are referred to as coupon payments on the bond.) To calculate the yield to maturity on the bond, R (at an annual rate), we use the NPV formula:

$$P_B = 200 = \frac{110}{(1 + R)} + \frac{121}{(1 + R)^2} \tag{7.1}$$

The value of R that equates the purchase price (£200) with the discounted present value of future coupon payments (£110 and £121) is (by convention) the yield to maturity. Here $R = 0.1$ or 10 per cent per annum. The investor can then loosely compare the annual yield over two years on the bond with the yield over one year on the bill R. Clearly, what happens to short-term (i.e. one-year bill) rates in the second year is of importance here and this aspect is dealt with when discussing the term structure of interest rates, below.

While the coupon payments on a bond are known with certainty over the remaining life of the bond, this is not the case for equities or common stocks. These assets usually pay a dividend, but the amount of the dividend is uncertain and depends in part upon the future level of profits. Hence it would be difficult to calculate a meaningful measure of the yield to maturity. In any case, there are several problems with the yield to maturity measure of the return, even for a bond. The most obvious is that it assumes a 'holding period' equal to the remaining life of the bond (i.e. until its redemption date) and the investor may have a shorter holding period. If the expected holding period is less than the life of the asset, then it makes more sense, particularly for long bonds, debentures and equities, to take account of expected capital gains over the holding period. Hence the holding period yield, HPY, is defined as:

$$HPY = [P_{t+1}^e - P_t + D_{t+1}]100/P_t \qquad (7.2)$$

where P_t = purchase price of the asset; P_{t+1}^e = expected price at the end of the (fixed and arbitrary) holding period (e.g. one year); and D_t+1 = any dividend or other payments made over the holding period. Thus, a corporate bond purchased for £90 with an expected dividend payment of £10 and an expected end-year price of £95 has a holding period yield of 16.7 per cent per annum. The latter is made up of an expected capital gain of 5.6 per cent and a dividend yield (D/P) 100 = 11.1 per cent. Clearly, if we have two risky assets, for example, an equity and a five-year bond and the holding period is one year, we would expect the holding period yield on both these assets to be above that on a risk-free asset (e.g. one-year term deposit in a bank). Of course, the HPYs on each risky asset are unlikely to be equal as equity is likely to be viewed as the riskier (e.g. risk of bankruptcy and uncertain dividend payments) and hence requires a higher HPY than the bond. However, we expect the HPY on each risky asset to rise and fall together so that the gap between the two HPYs is likely to remain reasonably constant over time.

We shall find it convenient to use the concept of the yield to maturity when discussing the yield curve and the HPY when discussing the investors' choice between bonds and equity. Note, however, that the HYP and the yield to maturity, R, on a bond may move together. For example, a fall in bond prices today (with an unchanged future price P_{t+1}^e) implies an increase in both the HPY (see (7.2)) and the yield to maturity R (see (7.1)). Space constraints prevent an analysis of the concept of the HPY in relation to the general problem of the pricing of all risky assets – this is done in the so-called capital asset pricing model or CAPM, which may be found in most introductory finance books.

Returning now to our main theme, we note that at any point in time a set of interest differentials will be established between bills and bonds, based on supply and demand in these markets. There will also be a differential between the HPY on government bonds, corporate bonds and equities, reflecting the different perceived risk characteristics of these assets. In 'normal' periods new flows on to the market (for example, via pension funds) will largely be allocated in much the same proportion as previous flows (Friedman 1977) and are unlikely to alter existing differentials radically.

Some short-term market interest rates are highly correlated with each other and interest differentials are small and remain constant. For example, commercial bills and three-month local authority bills are viewed as very close substitutes for banks' wholesale deposits and certificates of deposit. (Wholesale deposits are large-denomination fixed-term bank deposits made by companies, but cannot be 'sold'. Certificates of deposits are issued by banks when a company deposits funds and the company can then sell the 'certificate' on the stock exchange – although the new recipient cannot 'cash' it until the redemption/payment date.) Hence these three assets have almost identical interest rates, which move together.

Rates of interest on non-marketable assets such as building society deposits will also move with market rates to preserve differentials. For example, if local authority bill rates rise, and people begin switching out of bank and building society deposits into bills, these latter institutions will raise the rate on their deposits, for, if they fail to raise rates, they will have to contract their lucrative lending operations on bank and mortgage advances. However, as banks and building societies are now paying higher rates on deposits, to remain solvent or keep profits high they must raise the interest rate on new and existing advances. Hence changes in market rates spread to rates on non-marketable assets and liabilities. The spread between a bank's borrowing rate and its lending rate will vary depending upon the profitability of the bank and the economic cycle. In times of recession, when lending to companies is riskier and perhaps bank profits are low, the bank may widen the margin between its lending and borrowing rates.

The HPYs on bonds and equities will also tend to move together as investors buy and sell the two assets in order to (largely) preserve the

HPY differentials between them (assuming no change in the perceived riskiness of the two types of asset).

The businessman must continually be aware of the flows of funds through the market and will no doubt gain insights into short-term movements in relative rates and prices from the financial press and City contacts. The above intuitive ideas can also be examined with the aid of relatively complex financial models and to date only the London Business School (LBS) (Keating 1985b), HM Treasury (1982) and the Bank of England (Barr and Cuthbertson 1991) have a financial sector even remotely this complex. However, software for some of these models is now available on IBM-compatible personal computers.[2]

It should now be clear to the reader that a change in one financial market will, via the above mechanisms, have a ripple effect throughout the financial system. A major and frequent external source of changes in financial markets is operations by the Central Bank in pursuit of its monetary or exchange-rate policies. How do such policies affect interest rates and hence the investment decisions of firms? It is to this interaction between the Central Bank and the financial markets that we now turn.

7.3   INTEREST RATE DETERMINATION

In the previous section we noted that interest rates tend to broadly move together and for the most part tend to preserve interest differentials. The authorities may, for policy reasons, wish to control the overall level of interest rates or the growth in the money supply. Monetary targets have been instituted in recent years in a number of industrialized countries and attempts by the Central Bank to achieve these targets will lead to changes in interest rates. In fact, Central Banks tend to operate (i.e. buy and sell) mainly at the short end of the market when setting their monetary stance. Central Banks, for example, purchase vast quantities of three-month Treasury and commercial bills, some of which have only weeks or days to their maturity date. (In contrast, they tend to buy and sell in the long-term bond market (i.e. gilts or government bonds) only when demand is favourable.) As we see below, these operations at the 'short end' give the authorities a lever on the absolute level of key short-term interest rates, which may then alter long-term interest rates, bond and equity prices. This ripple effect through the financial system leads to changes in a whole host of interest rates and asset prices (and, indeed, in quantities held of different assets by the various financial institutions).

The Central Bank can operate a 'pure' financial transaction by buying or selling financial assets with members of the non-bank private sector (NBPS), that is, people, companies, building societies, LAPF or with the banks themselves. The reason we separate out 'sales' to the NBPS is that this has important implications for control of the money supply. However, fiscal policy involving changes in government expenditure and tax receipts is also usually accompanied by financial transactions because the Central Bank has an obligation to obtain finance for any debts the fiscal authorities may incur. The link between fiscal policy, the money supply and financing the government's debt is therefore a key factor in understanding movements in interest rates.

The public sector borrowing requirement (PSBR)

Crudely speaking, the difference between total expenditure by the government, G, and tax receipts, T, is known as the budget deficit or public sector borrowing requirement, PSBR.[3] The government must provide cash to finance any excess expenditure over tax receipts and this gives rise to the interdependence between fiscal and monetary policy. If, in a sense, the authorities do nothing after an increase in government expenditure (on, say, additional civil servants or a new road-building programme) they write out cheques drawn on the Bank of England. This by definition automatically increases the money supply (i.e. current accounts of the non-bank private sector, NBPS) as these cheques are presented to commercial banks like Lloyds and the National Westminster. Hence the interdependence of fiscal and monetary policy.

Can the authorities, when faced with a positive PSBR (i.e. $G-T \geq 0$), claw back the 'automatic' increase in the money supply and keep the money supply constant? The answer is yes, provided they are willing to raise interest rates enough to encourage some members of the NBPS to purchase additional (i.e. new issues of) government securities equal to the initial increase in the PSBR and hence also equal to the initial automatic increase in the money supply.

With a PSBR of £1 billion and hence an automatic increase in the money supply of £1 billion (for example, to civil servants) the authorities need to sell £1 billion of government debt (for example, Treasury bills or long-term bonds such as gilt-edged stock) to other members of the NBPS (for example, pension funds, which obtain their funds from personal sector savings). To encourage the NBPS to take up additional government bills (or bonds) the authorities must lower their market price or, what is the same thing, increase the interest rate on bills (or bonds).[4] Only then will pension funds switch out of money (i.e. current or deposit accounts) into bills. If the authorities wish to control the money supply (for example, keep it constant), they must be willing to see interest rates rise to the level that just encourages pension funds (and other members of the NBPS) to purchase £1 billion of government debt. This is the origin of the remark that if the authorities control the money supply they cannot simultaneously impose a particular interest rate. Thus, a cut in the money supply (compared to what it otherwise would have been) involves an increase in the overall level of interest rates. The authorities can, within reason, predict how much interest rates will rise, but they cannot prevent the rise if they wish to keep a constant money supply.

With a monetary target, therefore, an unforeseen increase in the PSBR is likely to lead to a higher interest rate on bills (for example, Treasury bills, commercial bills). Conversely, if the authorities reduce the PSBR (for example, by cutting welfare payments), while maintaining their monetary target, this is likely to result in a fall in interest rates, as the Central Bank has to sell fewer bills and bonds to the NBPS. This is why forecasts and out-turn for the PSBR are so keenly watched by the market-makers on the stock exchange. Indeed, with an element of forward-looking behaviour, as occurs with rational expectations (RE) (explained in Chapter 2), an announced cut in the PSBR, if believed by the market-makers, will result in an immediate fall in interest rates. This is because dealers on the stock exchange believe interest rates will fall in the future (that is, bond prices rise) as a consequence of a lower PSBR, in the future. However, only if they buy bonds today will brokers expect to make a profit in the future when bond prices actually do rise. But if all dealers buy today, the bond price rises today. Hence RE brings forward in time the effect of any announced policy changes. The lesson here for the businessman is to note the speed with which the market reacts to changes in or 'news' about new policies, if market-makers are forward looking in their behaviour. Interest-rate changes may precede the actual event that causes the change!

'Pure' monetary policy

In what follows, we shall in the main consider the money supply to be so-called 'broad money'. In the United Kingdom this, largely speaking, consists of cash plus current (chequing) accounts plus seven-day and other interest-bearing deposit accounts (for example, the large deposits by companies known as wholesale deposits or certificates of deposit) denominated in sterling and held by UK residents in banks based in the United Kingdom. (The analysis would remain valid if we included building societies in our definition of banks.) Although fiscal policy has monetary implications and therefore implications for the level of interest rates, the authorities can accomplish a change in the money supply without having to alter their fiscal policy. They do this by an open market sale or purchase of bonds to the NBPS and this is known as 'pure' monetary policy. For example, to reduce the money supply by £1 billion, the authorities sell £1 billion of government stock to the NBPS and to do so they need to increase interest rates (lower bond prices) to provide an incentive for the NBPS to switch out of money into government stock.

A rather subtle point here is that the Central Bank must sell or buy bonds from the NBPS and not from commercial banks if it is to have a direct effect on the money supply. If the Central Bank buys £100 million of commercial bills from a bank (for example, Lloyds), the bank loses £100 million of assets in the form of bills, but gains £100 million of balances at the Central Bank (which therefore acts as banker to the commercial banks). This is an example of asset switching by the commercial bank and there has been no direct change in the level of bank deposits held by the NBPS and hence, by definition, no direct change in the money supply. Of course, this is not to deny that now the commercial bank is more liquid it may on-lend these funds in higher bank advances to the NBPS, which creates a bank deposit for the NBPS and hence increases the money supply. This, however, is an indirect impact on the money supply and is discussed further below.

A policy of selling government debt to the NBPS will, as we saw above, lead to an initial, direct and automatic reduction in the money supply (i.e. cheque accounts). However, this is not the end of the matter because the commercial banks nowadays have a great deal of freedom to resist and circumvent the fall in business represented by this initial fall in deposits.

First, they can raise the interest they pay on wholesale deposits to attract more funds. However, *ceteris paribus*, this involves additional payments of interest by the commercial banks and to avoid a worsening on their profit and loss account they will probably raise their interest rates on bank advances, in order to increase their interest receipts per pound loaned out. The latter ought to encourage companies to reduce their outstanding overdrafts and advances, and hence the money supply.[5] Frequently, companies do not mind having large overdrafts if these are matched by wholesale deposits earning nearly as much interest. Hence the money supply depends on the interest rate on deposits relative to that on bank advances. But the authorities can only influence the absolute level of interest rates, not this relative rate, and hence they can only achieve imprecise control over the size of the broad money supply.[6]

In addition, a rise in the rate on bank lending leads to an automatic increase in the recorded level of advances and hence the money supply, as additional loan interest payments (owed) are added to the outstanding stock of advances. Also, to the extent that high interest rates are associated with a recession and a fall in the sales receipts of firms, firms will cover these short-term losses by increasing their overdrafts. Thus the authorities' control over the broad money supply via their use of open market operations and changes in interest rates is somewhat tenuous, particularly in the short-run. Nevertheless, it does appear that Central Banks can have a considerable influence on short-term interest rates and we now examine how this works through the rest of the financial system.

Ripple effect

By way of an example, consider the Central Bank selling existing short-term bills to the NBPS.[7] The market price of bills falls to encourage additional purchasers and hence short-term interest rates rise. The commercial banks initially lose bank deposits (i.e. money supply falls) as the cheques of the NBPS are payable to the Central Bank. In addition, the commercial banks' balances at the Central Bank fall when the Central Bank presents the cheque for payment to the commercial bank. As bankers' balances are reserve assets for the commercial banks, their reserves fall. As described above, the banks may then raise the interest rate on wholesale deposits and bank advances. The commercial bank may also try and sell its bills, to obtain cash to replenish its depleted reserves. However, as long as the Central Bank does not buy the bills sold by the banks, the reserves of the banks will remain at their lower level. (If the Central Bank bought bills from the banks, balances at the Central Bank would rise and reserves would be restored to their previous level.)

Now the banks as a whole are short of liquidity (reserves) and they have increased the interest rate on bank advances and bank deposits. If the rise in rates on advances reduces the demand for advances, as in the situation where firms use some of their bank deposits to pay off loans, the money supply falls even further. However, more interesting is that people will begin to switch funds out of low-yield building society deposits into high-yield bank deposits. To counter this loss of business, the building societies will raise their deposit rates and to remain solvent will raise their mortgage advance rates.

The higher rate on bills will lead some people to sell longer-term bonds (e.g. gilt-edged stock) in order to switch into high-yield bills. However, this causes bond prices to fall and hence long interest rates or more precisely the yields to maturity, R (equation 7.1), to rise. In addition, the holding period yield, HPY, on bonds may rise as the current price has fallen and the future price remains unchanged. Hence people will also now find it profitable to switch out of debentures and equity into high-yield long-term bonds. This leads to a fall in equity prices and a rise in their HPY. Thus, we see that a whole chain of interest-rate increases and a fall in equity prices has followed the initial rise in bill rates engineered by the Central Banks' open market operation. The absolute level of all interest rates rises. Bond and equity prices fall so that the HPY on these assets is brought back to equilibrium and any HPY differential is maintained.

The link between the rise in short rates and the long rate on fixed-interest long-term bonds is taken up further below when we discuss the yield curve. The link between changes in the absolute level of interest rates and the level of demand in the economy is discussed in Chapter 9. Clearly, a rise in interest rates on bank advances and a fall in equity prices increase the cost of borrowing for firms and are unlikely to result in a fall in expenditure on investment goods.

What about the impact on relative rates? Here it is very difficult to generalize as we have noted the strong interdependence between different financial markets. However, some progress on the link between short rates and long rates can be gained by examining the behaviour of the yield curve; a topic frequently discussed in the financial press.

Yield curve

The interest differential (or relative interest rate) between 'longs' and 'shorts' can be examined by combining our ideas of equilibrium in financial markets and the importance of expectations. The yield curve provides an analysis of how the actions of the Central Bank at the short end of the maturity spectrum can influence long-term bond interest rates.

The relationship between the short rate, r_t, and the current long-term rate, R_t, on bonds is known as the term structure of interest rates

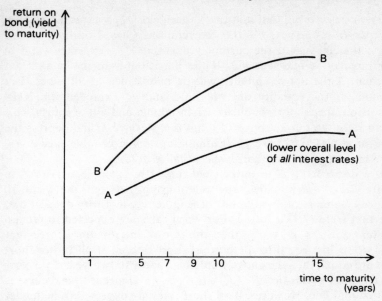

Figure 7.1 The yield curve
Note: For both curves, all expected short rates are assumed to be higher than current short rates

and gives rise to the yield curve. The yield curve shows the relationship between the interest rate on a bond (more precisely, the yield to maturity) and its time to maturity. Normally, the curve slopes upwards (AA in Figure 7.1) and becomes flatter as the time to maturity lengthens. A yield curve refers to a particular point in time (i.e. interest rates on a specific day) and the whole curve may shift up or down as the general level of all interest rates alters (BB Figure 7.1). The upward slope of the yield curve indicates, for example, that bonds with, say, twenty years to maturity will command a higher interest rate than those with one or two years to maturity. To understand the shape of the yield curve, consider the simple case of choosing between a three-year bond (i.e. one that matures in three years) and a series of three separate one-year investments in bills ('shorts'). If we ignore risk, then the investor will be indifferent between these two choices, if:

$$R_t^3 = \frac{1}{3} (r_t + {}_tr_{t+1}^e + {}_tr_{t+2}^e)$$

(7.3)

where R_t^3 = current annual (redemption) yield on a bond that matures in three years (which is known with certainty); r_t = current (known) interest rate on a bill that matures in one year; $_t r_{t+1}^e$ = expected yield in year two of a one-year bill (the expectation is based on information today, that is, year t, the current year); and $_t r_{t+2}^e$ = expected yield in year three on a one-year bill. If the participants in the market act 'efficiently', the above equality will be maintained at all times. For example, if the equality did not hold and R_t^3 exceeded the RHS expression, speculators would switch into longs and out of shorts. This would raise the market price of longs (i.e. lower R_t^3), and depress the price of shorts (i.e. raise r_t). Eliminating any profitable incentives, therefore, tends to re-establish the equality in (7.3).

How does (7.3) lead us to the yield curve (for example, curve AA in Figure 7.1), which shows the relationship between the yield to maturity (interest rate) on bonds of lengthening maturity dates? First, note that from (7.3) if future short-term rates are expected to remain constant, i.e. $r_t = _t r_{t+1}^e = _t r_{t+2}^e$, then the rate of interest on a three-year bond R_t^3, is just equal to the current short rate, r_t. If all future short rates are equal, then the above would also apply to two-year, four-year and five-year bonds (i.e. $R_t^2 = R_t^4 = R_t^5 = \ldots r_t$). Hence the yield curve is a horizontal line. However, if all short rates are expected to be higher in the future, i.e. $_t r_{t+2}^e \rangle _t r_{t+1}^e \rangle r_t$, then $R_t^3 \rangle r_t$ and the yield curve is the upward-sloping curve AA (Figure 7.1).

A downward-sloping yield curve occurs when future short rates are expected to be lower than the current short rate. This might be the case if inflation is expected to fall in the future as this will be reflected in lower future expected short rates. Also, if the monetary authorities use high short-term interest rates to deflate the economy (as in the UK in 1990–1) and this policy is expected to be reversed in the future, then future short-term rates are expected to fall and therefore long rates will be below short rates.

In practice, long bonds carry additional risk relative to bills. First, unless held to maturity their market price is uncertain. Second, even if held to maturity the real value of the interest payments (i.e. after deducting for inflation) may be far more uncertain on long bonds than on a series of one-year investments as future short rates are likely to broadly equal the rate of inflation pertaining in future periods. Thus, long rates will tend to be above short rates even if $_t r_{t+j}^e = r_t$ (for all j) because of this risk element.

The yield curve indicates that the authorities, by manipulating short rates, may have direct leverage over long rates on government stock. A rise in short rates may lead, via the term structure relationship (7.3), to a rise in long rates (i.e. upward shift of the yield curve) and a fall in bond prices. Lower bond prices today with unchanged expectations imply a higher holding-period yield (HPY) on bonds and hence a switch out of equities into bonds. Equity prices therefore fall until HPY rises in line with that on bonds. Hence, because long government bonds are reasonably close substitutes for debentures and equities, changes in government bond rates also influence debentures and equity returns.

Lower interest rates on gilt-edged stock, for example, imply a lower expected HPY. Equities and debentures now appear relatively more attractive and increased purchases lead to a rise in their market price. This makes it cheaper for firms to float new issues as they can obtain more cash per share issued. Hence the authorities, by operating on short rates, may influence a whole range of long rates of return, for example, on gilts and in a less predictable fashion influence the market price of debentures, preference shares and equities, and hence the cost of finance for firms raising money on the stock exchange.

We also noted above that the Central Bank's open market operations lead to changes in the cost of non-marketable assets such as the rate on bank advances. Hence, the Central Bank also has an indirect effect on the cost of finance for firms and this leads to changes in stock building (of raw materials, finished goods and work in progress) and fixed investment (in plant, machinery, buildings and vehicles). Thus, monetary policy can influence aggregate demand via its effect on the general level of a wide range of interest rates, an issue we take up in Chapter 9.

To summarize, the yield curve shows that the authorities can influence long rates via their operations at the short end of the market and this in turn is likely to influence the cost of finance for firms from debenture and preference shares or issues of new equity. Note that even if the firm uses retained profits to finance its real investment expenditure, changes in market interest rates will still influence investment decisions. This is because one alternative to real investment is investment in marketable financial assets (for example, gilt-edged stock, other firms' equity). The higher the yield on the latter, the less likely it is that retained profits will be used by the firm to increase its own real investment expenditures.

Other influences

We have now discussed the main domestic factors that influence interest rates and we turn briefly to discuss influences that arise from the foreign sector (capital account), expectations and risk.

As we noted in Chapter 6, the United Kingdom economy is subject to capital flows that impinge on UK interest rates. A useful starting point is to assume uncovered interest parity, UIP, but to include a (percentage) risk factor, θ, in this relationship:

$$r = r^* + \mu + \theta \qquad (7.4)$$

This simply states that, for speculators to be indifferent between domestic and foreign assets, the domestic interest rate, r, must be equal to the expected return on holding foreign assets, $(r^* + \mu)$, plus an adjustment for risk, θ. The return to investing in the foreign asset consists of the foreign interest rate, r^*, plus the expected appreciation of the foreign currency, μ. Thus, if the UK is the domestic economy and the USA the foreign economy, the return to a UK resident of investing in the USA is the US interest rate, r^*, plus the (percentage) rise in the dollar against sterling, expected to occur over the holding period. Because future exchange-rate movements are uncertain, the UK resident may require a return on US assets that is higher than the known return on UK assets before he is willing to invest in the USA. Thus, UK interest rates may be less than the uncertain foreign return, $(r^* + \mu)$, and this will not result in any outflow of funds from the UK (i.e. $\theta < 0$).

In reality, there are many risks to investing in foreign assets. For example, on foreign bonds there are institutional risks, such as risk of default, bankruptcy and the possible imposition of exchange controls. For investment in foreign equities or common stocks there is risk concerning the variability of returns on the foreign stock market, as well as risk due to movements of the exchange rate.

Often the monetary authorities raise short-term interest rates to curtail excessive growth in domestic demand. The rise in domestic rates (if unanticipated) will attract a foreign capital inflow and put upward pressure on the exchange rate. In fact, in the model of section 6.3, the exchange rate initially overshoots its long-run value. It is the impact of an appreciation in the domestic currency on net trade and aggregate demand that often leads governments to abandon adherence to a tight monetary stance.

The uncovered parity (UIP) condition, together with a risk premium, provides a useful starting point for the analysis of open economy factors that influence domestic interest rates. From 7.4 it is clear that foreign interest rates, r^*, are likely to influence domestic interest rates: a rise in US rates due, for example, to a tight monetary policy by the Federal Reserve Board will tend to lead to a capital outflow from the domestic (UK) economy; bond prices in the UK fall and domestic interest rates rise, which tends to restore UIP. Note that with rational expectations (RE) a rise in domestic rates might occur at the time of the announcement of a tight US monetary policy, rather than when the actual money supply in the USA is cut.

A negative differential between UK and US interest rates can ensue (i.e. $r - r^* < 0$) if foreign-exchange speculators expect sterling to appreciate in the future (i.e. $\mu < 0$). The most obvious recent factor here is the discovery of North Sea oil and the rise in the world price of oil. These factors imply a strong UK oil balance in the future and FOREX dealers will expect sterling to appreciate. This may have allowed UK interest rates to fall relative to world interest rates in the 1980s.

Perceptions of risk can also drive a wedge between domestic and foreign interest rates. For example, even if FOREX dealers expect no change in the exchange rate ($\mu = 0$), UK interest rates may still be below US rates, ($r < r^*$), if speculators think the risk attached to their expectation (of $\mu = 0$) has fallen (perhaps due to a firm credible commitment announced by the government to maintain the existing exchange rate). While such market sentiment is difficult to quantify, it nevertheless impinges on UK interest rates, particularly in the short term. If we broaden the UIP relationship so that it applies to uncertain capital assets (e.g. equities and long bonds), then r and r* are replaced by expected HPYs (on UK and US equities, say). In this case the expected HPY on UK equities may be below that on US equities because the former is perceived as less risky, perhaps because the variability in UK company profits, which directly influences the variability of UK equity prices, is perceived to be relatively small. (To analyse this issue further requires use of the so-called international CAPM.)

Like the exchange rate, day-to-day movements in interest rates are dominated by news or unanticipated events and this is what makes interest rates so volatile. Announcements about UK or foreign monetary and fiscal policy will be quickly assimilated by market-makers in the global money markets and reflected in new quoted interest rates. However, for most business decisions a longer-term view of interest-rate development is probably more important than these short-term movements due to news which may be quickly reversed.

7.4 FORECASTING INTEREST RATES

As noted above, movements in interest rates over the very short term are not capable of being forecast as such movements are dominated by new information or news. In addition, very short-term *expectations* will influence day-to-day movements in interest rates. To give an example, it was widely expected that (short-term) UK interest rates would fall by half a per cent (or more) on budget day in April 1987. Market-makers, therefore, borrowed heavily in the overnight interbank market, pushing this borrowing rate up to around 35 per cent (at an annual rate). They used the proceeds to purchase (say) three-month commercial bills (with a yield of about 9.5 per cent). On budget day, interest rates did fall by 0.5 per cent, that is, the market price of commercial bills rose. Market-makers then sold their bills, after holding them overnight, and used the capital gain to pay off the overnight interbank loan and make a profit on the deal. In this case, short-term expectations increased a key market rate, namely interbank rate, by a substantial amount. This behaviour is, in the main, unpredictable.

Over the medium and longer term (say three months to one year and one to five years respectively) we can obtain some insights into the future movements in interest rates. However, no forecast of interest rates can ever be anything more than an informed guess, but this may be better than an uninformed one.

A useful starting point is to consider what are the fundamental long-run forces affecting domestic UK interest rates. Uncovered interest parity indicates that the domestic interest rate, r, should equal the foreign interest rate, r*, plus the expected appreciation in the foreign currency, μ, plus an adjustment for risk, θ:

$$r = r^* + \mu + \theta \tag{7.5}$$

What, then, is likely to influence the expected depreciation of (say) sterling in the long run (i.e. an appreciation in the foreign currency)? Clearly the current account must balance in the longer term and broadly speaking this requires the domestic inflation rate to equal the foreign rate. (This is simply asserting long-run PPP.) Hence in the long run any forecast of interest rates must be based on:

1 forecasts of foreign interest rates, r*, especially US and German interest rates. These will be influenced by the monetary stance of the Federal Reserve Board and the Bundesbank. An overshoot in, say, US monetary targets can be expected to be followed by a rise in US rates and hence UK rates of interest;
2 forecasts of relative inflation rates. The higher expected domestic inflation is or the faster inflation rises, then the greater the expected depreciation in sterling and the higher United Kingdom interest rates are likely to be; and

3 the relative attractiveness of the domestic economy as reflected in the risk premium θ. This is difficult to quantify, but clearly perceived 'sound' government policies, the overall productivity of the economy and inward (net) direct investment by foreign companies are indicative of a 'strong' economy. In the case of the United Kingdom, increased North Sea oil output and the price of oil also reduce the perceived riskiness of investing in the UK relative to the US.

Over the medium term there are additional factors that need to be taken into account when forecasting interest rates. The most important of these is the policy stance of the government. If the authorities have a monetary target, then any monetary growth in excess of the target range is likely to be met by a rise in interest rates by the Central Bank. For similar reasons, an overshoot in a PSBR target is also likely to result in the authorities financing this, in part, by future sales of government bonds, which will also raise interest rates.

Institutional changes can also impinge upon interest rates, particularly relative rates. Businessmen have to keep a watchful eye on such developments as they directly impinge upon the cost of borrowing. These changes generally come under the heading of financial innovation. For example, in the UK in the early 1980s, after the introduction of more competition in the banking sector (i.e. competition and credit control) and among building societies post 1986, the interest differential between the borrowing rates and lending rates in these institutions narrowed. In the case of the former, this attracted company treasurers to borrow relatively more via bank advances (rather than directly on the stock exchange) as well as to hold a high buffer stock of high-yielding liquid assets. Relaxation of credit controls on personal sector borrowing led to a substantial sharp rise in the debt–income ratio of people. Financial innovation and the ending of UK exchange controls in 1979 also led to a greater integration of domestic and overseas financial markets (for example, the Eurocurrency markets) and a plethora of new financial instruments (for example, floating rate notes, currency swaps, etc). This has meant that over the medium term the impact of foreign interest rates on domestic interest rates has been quicker and more potent. In forecasting, this implies that the businessman may need to have a global view of developments in international capital markets if he is to fully comprehend and attempt to forecast UK interest rates.

In Chapter 9 we further discuss the impact of monetary and fiscal policy on domestic interest rates, within the context of a complete macroeconomic model.

7.5   SUMMARY

In this chapter we have discussed the main sources and uses of funds within the domestic financial system. The huge flow of funds between financial institutions leads to the establishment of particular interest differentials or relative rates of return between different assets. These relative yields are influenced by the forces of supply and demand between the various markets and also by the actions of the monetary authorities.

The Central Bank can influence certain key interest rates by buying and selling assets (bills or long-term government bonds) in the market. This then has a ripple effect on other interest rates within the system and may lead to changes in the overall level of all interest rates, as well as changes in some interest differentials within the system. The authorities' impact on the absolute level of rates is far easier to predict than their impact on relative rates. Expectations, foreign interest rates and perceptions of risk can also have as major impact on domestic interest rates. Perhaps the most important linkage is between UK and US and German short-term interest rates: unless exchange-rate expectations alter, changes in these interest rates have a very strong impact on UK rates. Largely extraneous factors (for example, oil price rises) can also affect UK interest rates as they alter foreigners' perceptions of the general level of risk in investing in UK companies (the 'strong economy factor') or FOREX dealers' views about the expected change in the exchange rate. Both these effects work via the uncovered interest parity relationship.

The reader must obviously be aware of the high degree of volatility in financial markets: interest rates, bond and equity prices, and exchange rates can undergo very substantial changes over short periods. One question that arises is whether such movements are the result of actions by rational agents based on economic fundamentals or whether they are heavily influenced by whim and caprice.

At present this appears to be an open question. There is evidence to support the view that some financial markets (e.g. stock markets) are excessively volatile and this may be due to fads or speculative bubbles (e.g. South Sea Bubble). For example, it is difficult to see what major changes in economic fundamentals (e.g. forecasts of dividends) could have occurred in the week of 19 October 1987 ('Black Monday') to cause the world's stock markets to crash by over 30 per cent. Evidence and new theoretical models are beginning to appear in the literature that suggest that herding behaviour could play a major role in determining fluctuations in financial markets in particular periods. If correct, and stock prices are not based on economic fundamentals, then there is a possible rationale for government intervention in the market. The latter has always been a hotly debated issue in the market for foreign exchange where governments have over substantial periods tried to influence the exchange rate (e.g. the Plaza and Louvre Agreements of the late 1980s on stabilizing exchange rates of the major industrialized (G7) countries and the setting up of the exchange rate mechanism, ERM; see Chapter 9). Also, as we have seen, governments do not usually leave the movement of interest rates solely to market forces, but intervene via active open market operations.

Thus if asset prices such as interest rates and exchange rates left solely to market forces produce excess volatility and undesirable macroeconomic effects, the authorities may damp down such movements by announcing bands and target ranges for these variables.

To repeat, the importance of the future course of interest rates is of obvious importance for the solvency and future investment plans of individual firms. In this chapter we hope we have dealt with the main macroeconomic forces that impinge upon interest rates (and other asset prices) so that the businessman can analyse the material in the financial press and on government policy.

NOTES

1 There is always an implicit interest paid on chequing accounts equal to the manpower and capital costs of administering these accounts.
2 The address is EFU, London Business School, Sussex Place, Regent's Park, London NW1.
3 Strictly speaking we shall be discussing changes in the budget deficit. However, we shall use the more popular term PSBR. Broadly speaking, the two classifications differ in that asset sales (for example, British Gas, British Airways) by the government affect the PSBR but not the budget deficit.
4 See note 1, Chapter 6.
5 A fall in advances (*ceteris paribus*) automatically leads to a fall in deposits and hence the money supply in the bank in question. It is perhaps easiest to see this by considering what happens when a bank grants an advance to a firm: bank deposits (initially the chequing account) of the firm increase as do the 'assets side' of the bank's balance sheet (since the advance must be paid back eventually). After the firm has spent the advance its bank deposit falls and that of another member of the NBPS increases. To pay back its advance the firm must increase its receipts and eventually place these in its current account. When its current account equals the amount of the initial advance the firm 'pays back' its advance and its current account (i.e. the

money supply) falls by an equal amount. (See Cuthbertson 1979 for further details.)

6 At times in the early 1970s United Kingdom banks offered a higher return on wholesale deposits to large firms than they were charging on overdrafts and advances. Hence firms borrowed from one bank on overdraft to invest in wholesale deposits in another bank. This was known as 'round tripping' and substantially increased the growth in £M3. (See Cuthbertson 1984 and Cuthbertson 1986 for further details.)

7 Since the 'new monetary arrangements' of 1981 the Bank of England has dealt in commercial bills rather than Treasury bills. In order to supply liquidity (cash) to the banks it has purchased large quantities of commercial bills from them. A bill mountain has therefore emerged – a non-EEC mountain in this case!

8 Wages and prices

There are a number of reasons why firms are interested in the general level of prices. One is that the price set by an individual firm for the year ahead and its wage negotiations clearly depend in part upon what it believes the general rate of wage and price inflation will be. It is costly to alter prices frequently (loss of goodwill, possible switching by previously loyal customers, cost of new brochures and price lists, etc.) and wage negotiations often swallow up scarce managerial time. In Chapters 5 and 7 we discussed the importance of interest rates in determining a firm's investment decisions. If we use a nominal interest rate (i.e. as quoted by a bank or on the stock exchange) to discount future profit streams in our NPV calculation (see Chapter 3) then this may have to be adjusted to take account of future inflation. A higher expected rate of inflation implies higher nominal interest rates in the future, as loans are 'rolled over'. Hence inflation forecasts are crucial not only in calculating net future profits but also in choosing the future interest rate at which to discount these profit streams. It is, therefore, important to make use of all the macro information available to improve decision-making in this area.

A second reason is that inflation has become an important issue in its own right, to the extent that it is now a major target of government policy. Governments often exhort firms to be resistant to high wage claims because of their impact upon prices. For these reasons alone, the businessman will want to know both how prices are determined and how they may be forecast. We begin with a look at theoretical relationships determining prices and inflation – a natural extension of our analyses of Chapter 2. In section 8.2 we move on to consider the wage–price interaction in more detail and introduce a further important element in the inflation story, namely the exchange rate.

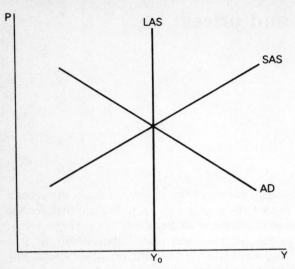

Figure 8.1 Aggregate demand and supply as a function of the price level

8.1   THE DETERMINATION OF PRICES

We have already examined, in Chapter 4, the relationship between
output and the price level, P, and we now extend that analysis to the
rate of inflation, Δp (i.e. changes in the price level). It was argued in
Chapter 2 that aggregate demand was negatively related to the level of
prices and a mainstream view would be that the aggregate supply
curve is upward sloping in the short run and (more controversially)
vertical in the long run. These relationships are depicted in Figure 8.1,
where LAS and SAS are the long- and short-run supply curves.

It is possible to redraw Figure 8.1 with the rate of inflation on the
vertical axis. Ther reason is that, at any given time, an increase in the
inflation rate ensures a higher price level than there would otherwise
have been. The implied relationship between inflation and output is
shown in Figure 8.2.[1]

The point Y_0 is defined in monetarist and neo-classical parlance as
the natural rate of output. It is natural in the sense that it is the rate at
which aggregate supply equals aggregate demand in the long run. We
now show why. For simplicity, assume that in the absence of
productivity growth the monetarists are correct in believing that in the
long run the rate of change of prices will be equal to the rate of change
of the money supply. Assume that this is 12 per cent and that we begin
in equilibrium at point A in Figure 8.3. Let us now assume that the

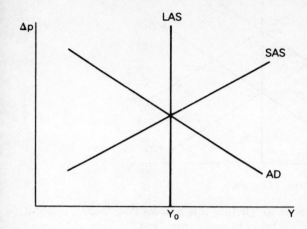

Figure 8.2 Aggregate demand and supply as a function of the rate of inflation

government feels that 12 per cent is too high a rate of inflation and cuts the money supply growth rate to 5 per cent. As the growth of the money stock is now lower than the rate of inflation, the purchasing power of the money stock falls, people feel less wealthy and the aggregate demand curve shifts to the left. It falls, in fact, until it cuts the LAS curve at 5 per cent, for it it did not there would be a fall in the purchasing power of the money stock and we would be unable to maintain demand at Y_0. Thus inflation has to fall to 5 per cent to restore equilibrium in the long run.

The problem is that, even in monetarist models, we do not move straight to a point like C, but instead move down the short run SAS curve to point B. What happens there depends upon workers and their expectations. At point B inflation has fallen, but so has output and this implies an increase in unemployment. If there is a natural rate of unemployment, U_0, corresponding to the natural rate of output, Y_0, unemployment is now above the natural rate. In theory, what should now happen is that the real wage should fall, that firms' profits should, therefore, rise and that they will therefore wish to supply more; i.e. the short-run aggregate supply, SAS, shifts to the right (to SAS_1). Equilibrium is reached at point C, as illustrated in Figure 8.3. Should this occur, the outcome is permanently lower inflation at the expense of temporarily higher unemployment.

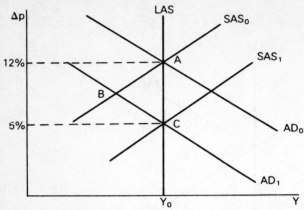

Figure 8.3 The actual rate of output

There are questions as to whether this process does occur, and if it does, the length of time it takes to move from B to C.[2] This will depend upon the following factors:

1 inflationary expectations. The quicker these adjust, the lower money wage demands and hence real wages will be. The lower the latter are, the lower firms' costs will be and the more they may wish to supply;
2 real wages. The more responsive these are to higher unemployment, the faster firms' costs should fall and the quicker output supplied increases; and
3 the extent to which firms do increase output as a result of a fall in costs.

In practice, doubt may be cast upon the extent to which each of the above will occur, so that the economy may be locked at a point like B for a considerable time. Indeed, it may stay there for so long that some workers become unemployable so that potential or natural output and the LAS curve shift back towards point B.

In any event, as the UK evidence shows, economies can get stuck for considerable periods at points like B, suggesting that monetarist remedies for inflation are far less simple than originally supposed.

There are perhaps two issues that we should explore further.

An expansion of aggregate demand

Assume we begin at point C in Figure 8.4 and that the government decides that the level of unemployment, U_0, corresponding to Y_0 is too

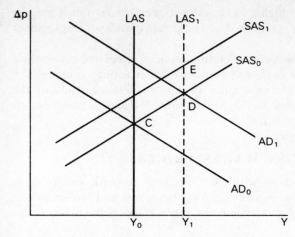

Figure 8.4 An expansion of aggregate demand

high. It therefore expands demand by an increase in the growth of the money supply. We now move to a point D on SAS_0 (Figure 8.4). If the monetarists are correct, the curve will then begin to shift to the left and unemployment will start to rise again. The only way the government can stop this is to keep expanding the money supply, so we move to a point E on the new SAS curve.

The net result, of course, is accelerating inflation. It follows, therefore, that attempts to keep unemployment below the natural rate cause permanently accelerating inflation in the monetarist view. For these reasons, U_0 (corresponding to Y_0) is described as the non-accelerating inflation rate of unemployment, NAIRU. As we argued in Chapter 2, a shift in LAS to LAS_1 (through D) is an alternative possibility and this requires vigorous supply-side policies such as tax incentives, improved training, infrastructure and productivity.

A rise in non-wage costs

A case in point here is the oil-price rise of the early 1970s, which increased firms' costs and reduced profits in the non-oil exporting countries. If we return to Figure 8.3 this is depicted by a movement from C to B, as firms wish to supply less at a given rate of inflation. Two possibilities now exist for a return to Y_0. One is for a fall in wage costs to mitigate against the rise in oil costs so that SAS shifts back to C. A second is that, in these circumstances, a government should expand aggregate demand so that we end up at point A. The inflationary costs are higher in the latter circumstance, but it may be argued that a quicker return to the natural rate of output/employment is thereby ensured.

This outlines the theoretical determination of prices and shows their interrelationship with fiscal and monetary policy acting via changes in aggregate demand. We now move to a more detailed study of the wage–price inflationary spiral, which provides a possible route to forecasting the rate of inflation.

8.2   FORECASTING WAGES/PRICES

The above analysis deals with the impact of domestic events upon inflation; it ignores the impact of the exchange rate and foreign prices. This closed-economy model may be represented mathematically as follows:

$$\Delta p = \beta_0 \, (Y - Y_0) + \beta_1 \Delta p^e + \beta_2 Z \qquad (8.1)$$

where Y_0 is the natural rate of output, Δp^e is the expected rate of inflation and Z is a catch-all variable representing, for example, trade union militancy or wage push and managerial efficiency factors.

In actual macroeconomic forecasting models, a more complex version is normally used separating prices and wages. This is now outlined.

In most 'mainstream' models, factory-gate prices (i.e. before any indirect taxes such as VAT are considered) are usually assumed to be determined by a fixed mark-up, K, over unit costs, UC:

$$P = K(UC) \qquad (8.2)$$

This suggests a dynamic model of the type:

$$\Delta p = \dot{UC} = \alpha(\Delta w - x_p) + (1 - \alpha) \, (\Delta p^* - \Delta s) \qquad (8.3)$$

The percentage change in unit costs, $\dot{UC}$, is a weighted average of wage costs (i.e. nominal wage increases, Δw, less the growth in labour productivity, x_p) and raw material costs (i.e. import prices in sterling). The weight, α, for the manufacturing sector is about 0.6–0.7, reflecting the relatively high proportion of wage costs in total costs. Indirect taxes would be added to (8.3) to obtain retail prices (we ignore this factor).

Wage increases are determined by a price expectations augmented Phillips curve (PEAPC). This is analogous to our theoretical discussion and to (8.1) except for the fact that it is couched in terms of unemployment (and the NAIRU, U_0) instead of output.

Here, wage inflation, Δw, increases either as unemployment, U, falls (i.e. excess demand for labour increases and AD shifts outwards) or when workers expect higher price inflation:

$$\Delta w = -f(U-U_0) + \beta\Delta p^e + x_w + Z \qquad (8.4)$$

x_w reflects wage increases due to productivity improvements and Z is as defined above.

Equations (8.3) and (8.4) embody a wage–price spiral. For example, a fall in unemployment below U_0 leads to higher wage claims as the labour market becomes 'tight', and this in turn leads to higher prices. The latter then feed back into higher wage claims and so on. A similar scenario ensues when a rise in sterling import prices, caused either by a rise in foreign prices, Δp^*, or a fall in the exchange rate (i.e. rise in s), increases domestic prices. Is this process stable in the same sense that inflation settles down to a new higher rate?

To examine this question, substitute for Δw from (8.4) in (8.3) (and assume $x_p = x_w$ for simplicity):

$$\Delta p = -\alpha f(U-U_0) + \alpha\beta\Delta p^e + \alpha Z + (1-\alpha)(\Delta p^* - \Delta s) \qquad (8.5)$$

We now wish to add two further assumptions to our wage–price sub-model. First, we make the reasonable assumption that when inflation is constant (i.e. non-accelerating) the economic agents' expectation of inflation equals the actual rate of inflation, $\Delta p = \Delta p^e$. Second, assume that workers do not suffer from money illusion and, therefore, they eventually gain full compensation for price increases. Thus, $\beta = 1$. From (8.5) we then have:

$$\Delta p = \frac{-\alpha f}{1-\alpha}(U-U_0) + \frac{\alpha}{1-\alpha}Z + (\Delta p^* - \Delta s) \qquad (8.6)$$

Equation (8.6) is the 'open-economy' (i.e. including exchange rates and world price effects) equivalent of equation (8.1). The only difference between them is the use of $(Y-Y_0)$ in (8.1) and $(U-U_0)$ in (8.6), and the latter incorporates the open-economy effects in the variable, $(\Delta p^* - \Delta s)$. Thus, our analysis in section 8.1 and the current discussion may be seen as complementary. Section 8.1 highlighted the impact of monetary and fiscal policy on $(Y-Y_0)$, which in turn implies changes in $(U-U_0)$. Shifts in the aggregate supply curve may be viewed as operating via the 'catch-all' Z variable. Thus, a major chain of causation is from monetary and fiscal policy via excess demand $(Y-Y_0$ or $U-U_0)$ and hence to the wage–price spiral embodied in (8.6). To the extent that monetary and fiscal policy have a direct impact on the exchange rate, this will also lead to a wage–price interaction via the term (Δp^* - Δs). How, then, does our theory of the wage–price interaction explain the differing forecasts of inflation produced by rival 'mainstream' forecasting groups (for example, HM Treasury, Bank of England, National Institute, London Business School)? A 1 per cent rise in all 'foreign prices' (for example, oil and raw materials) or a 1 per cent devaluation of sterling (the 'domestic' currency) eventually leads to a 1 per cent rise in domestic prices. Hence, inflation can be 'imported' and a devaluation is also inflationary.

It is worth digressing slightly to consider the implications of (8.6) for the balance of trade. A devaluation does not, in the long-run, alter the level of price competitiveness [p–(p^* – s)]. Therefore, there is no expenditure switching (i.e. increase in exports and decrease in imports) and no improvement (from this source) in the balance of payments position (see section 5.2). Of course, in the short run domestic prices rise less than the devaluation and there is some short-run improvement in the payments position due to expenditure switching. Equation (8.5) provides a wage–price model that implies that under 'fixed' exchange rates a devaluation does not, in the long run improve the payments position due to expenditure switching alone. Therefore, other factors are needed as an adjunct to the devaluation. These might include deflationary policies that increase unemployment (and hence reduce imports, for example). Deflation may arise automatically, if, after the devaluation, wages rise less than prices (in the short run), thus reducing real income and consumption, or if savings increase as inflation rises or if welfare payments do not keep pace with inflation. Induced deflation will have a direct effect on the payments position by reducing import volume.

Returning to our main theme of inflation, differing lag responses in different models are likely to be a major source of differences in inflation forecasts by rival groups over, say, a two-year horizon and, of course, indexing rates of specific duty (on alcohol and tobacco) can also add to consumer price increases. Note that the above discussion has only highlighted the proximate causes of inflation and there are additional feedbacks that can only be analysed using a 'full model'. For example, a rise in inflation caused by a rise in foreign prices might lead to a fall in consumers' expenditure, as people attempt to rebuild their savings which have been cut in real terms (Davidson *et al.* 1978)[3] This, in turn, will affect aggregate demand and unemployment and hence feedback into price inflation. These feedbacks are dealt with in the next chapter.

Finally, forecasters may use 'add factors' (or residual adjustments) in their price and wage equations. If, for example, forecasters believe that firms will use a 'boom period' to rebuild profit margins they will add a positive residual to the price equation (which is derived under the assumption of constant profit margins, where k = the constant mark-up) if an expansion of output is initially forecast.

So, to summarize, different inflation forecasts by rival (mainstream) groups may be due to:

1 different forecasts of external factors such as raw material prices;
2 different monetary and fiscal policies, which give rise to different levels of domestic excess demand (i.e. $U-U_0$);
3 different 'add factors' or push factors (Z) on wages;
4 different forecasts of exchange rates; and
5 differing views about lag responses or the speed with which workers adjust (and act on) their views about future price inflation.

Of course, these factors will also influence the businessman's own view of future inflation prospects.

NOTES

1 We are grateful to John Maloney for the simple exposition given here.
2 In rational expectations models with flexible prices the movement from A to C would be almost instantaneous if the cut in money supply were correctly perceived by the private sector.
3 If one has L_{t-1} = £100 in a bank deposit account earning r = 0.05 (5 per cent) p.a., then at the end of the year one's *nominal* assets are £105 (i.e. L_{t-1} $(1 + r)$). If inflation through the year was Δp = 0.1 (10 per cent) then the real purchasing power of one's assets is £105/1.1 = £95.4: one can buy about 5 per cent less goods at the end of the year than one could buy at the beginning. The 'inflation loss' on one's stock of savings (i.e. bank deposits) may result in lower consumption (next year) in order to partly rebuild these assets. In general, the change in real wealth is given by $(r - \Delta p)(L/P)_{t-1}$ where P = the aggregate price level, $(L/P)_{t-1}$ is initial real wealth. Thus, the real value of assets is eroded if the real interest rate $(r - \Delta p)$ is negative (i.e. $\Delta p > r$).

9 Monetary and fiscal policy and the European Monetary System

The importance of policy changes in altering key variables such as exchange rates, interest rates and the price level has already been partly examined by taking each variable largely in isolation. We now wish to discuss fiscal and monetary policy in some detail and explicitly to take account of the feedbacks and interactions between these key variables. Only then can we ascertain the full impact of policy changes on the macroeconomy. Fiscal policy working through the PSBR has implications for monetary policy, as argued in Chapter 7, but to simplify matters we first present the transmission mechanisms of the two major policy choices as if they were independent sequential events. We are then in a position to consider the net effects of these policies on, say, output and inflation. This is made more concrete by examining the simulation properties of 'real world' econometric models. In the final section we examine the macroeconomic aspects of the European Monetary System.

9.1 THEORETICAL ASPECTS

Initially, it is useful to concentrate on the effects of fiscal and monetary policy on aggregate demand in a closed economy. If we then add an assumption about the supply of labour and output (for example, the PEAPC) we can discuss the impact of monetary and fiscal policy on prices as well as output. Finally, after introducing the added complications of the open economy, namely trade and capital account flows, we can give a more complete picture. Thus, the previous chapters provide the basic building blocks for analysing fiscal and monetary policy. Our aim in what follows is to provide a guide to the businessman in interpreting the forecasts of rival groups. In this section we begin by discussing the qualitative impact of policy, which provides the groundwork for our quantitive illustrations in the next section.

We deal first with the main chain of causation (transmission mechanisms) of monetary policy. We then discuss fiscal policy and finally we draw on some issues specifically raised by the rational expectations hypothesis.

Monetary policy

We noted in Chapter 7 that the initial impact of open market operations is felt on short-term interest rates. The latter may then have a ripple effect on a number of interest rates in the financial system as people, pension funds, banks and the like switch between various assets. The most obvious link from monetary policy to expenditure on goods occurs through changes in interest-sensitive expenditures such as stock-building and fixed investment in plant, machinery and vehicles. In theoretical models (for example, Jorgenson 1971) it is usually the case that real investment (in plant and machinery or buildings) depends largely upon the real rate of interest.[1] However, in econometric work in the United Kingdom it has been difficult to isolate the impact of the rate of interest on investment expenditures (Hall *et al.* 1986, Holly and Longbottom 1985), perhaps because the effect of changes in interest rates working via 'front-end loading' (i.e. gearing or liquidity) constraints may be difficult to pick up. A firm may face a liquidity constraint because after taking out a new loan the firm's interest cost will be high. In fact, all its early repayments will be paying interest charges only and not the capital sum outstanding (as in the purchase of a house on a new mortgage). Banks, as a baseline, require loan interest payments to be always met. A rise in the general level of interest rates will often be accompanied by a minor recession and hence lower sales receipts. The firm may then have difficulty in meeting interest payments from sales revenue. This 'liquidity effect' may be the channel by which changes in interest rates influence investment expenditures.

In any event, there are other channels for monetary policy. One is that a rise in the cost of borrowing may reduce consumers' expenditure on non-durable goods (Hendry 1983) and particularly durable goods such as cars and electrical goods (Cuthbertson 1980). Further, a rise in interest rates implies a fall in bond prices and, in general, a fall in the all-share index on the stock exchange. This fall in wealth of the personal sector may also lead to a fall in consumers' expenditure (Pesaran and Evans 1984). These effects have been found to have relatively powerful effects on consumption.

We have already dealt with the impact of monetary policy (i.e.

change in interest rates or the money supply) upon the exchange rate and hence upon net export volume and aggregate demand. In UK models this transmission mechanism (whether or not it involves overshooting) is probably the most powerful and quick acting of all the monetary policy channels, as we see below.

The effects of monetary policy upon inflation work in two main ways. First, an increase in aggregate demand leads to a wage–price spiral via the excess demand term (for example, unemployment) in the Phillips curve. Second, a change in the exchange rate has a direct effect on (sterling) import prices and, hence, domestic costs and prices.

Inflation may then have further feedbacks on aggregate demand, which tend to attentuate the inflation. For example, a higher rate of inflation leads to a loss in the purchasing power of one's savings (wealth).[2] If people then save more to rebuild their financial assets (Hendry 1983, Cuthbertson 1982, 1983) they must consume less and hence aggregate demand falls back and via the Phillips curve inflation is attentuated.

The net effect of a change in monetary policy on output and inflation can, in general, only be ascertained using a complete macro-model. However, in one very important case, namely the 'neutrality of money', a 1 per cent change in the money supply leads to a 1 per cent change in prices and no change in real output. (This occurs when the demand for money is proportional to the price level, we have a vertical long-run aggregate supply curve and no wealth effects.)[3] However, it must be remembered that this widely quoted neo-classical result requires unchanging behavioural relationships over a long period of time as it is widely recognized that the neutrality result may take ten to fifteen years (Tobin 1981) to fully work itself through the economy.[4] It is perhaps prudent for the businessman to see the long run as a succession of short runs where monetary policy has strong effects on real output as well as inflation. Monetary policy, therefore, influences aggregate demand and inflation primarily through changes in interest-sensitive expenditures, and via exchange-rate effects on net trade flows and import prices.

Fiscal policy

We take fiscal policy to consist of a change in government expenditure on goods and services, G (for example, school building, road building), or a change in tax rates and tax receipts, T (unemployment and social security payments we can consider as negative taxes). Again, first we consider the effects of fiscal policy in a closed economy[5] and then introduce open economy aspects before dealing finally with inflationary consequences.

A cut in government expenditure leads to a (reverse) multiplier effect and a fall in aggregate demand. However, a fall in consumption (of durables), investment and stock building leads to a fall in the demand for bank advances by companies and people. This is likely to lead to a fall in interest rates on bank advances as the banks attempt to maintain their loan business. Firms also raise less money, thus issuing fewer corporate bonds, the price of which then rises (a cut in supply) and interest rates fall. The latter tends to increase investment and consumption (via a revaluation of wealth held in bonds), thus offsetting some of the initial fall in aggregate demand. In the short run, however, the net effect is a fall in aggregate demand.

We noted in section 7.3 that fiscal and monetary policy are interdependent. A cut in government expenditure causes a smaller fall in (income) tax receipts and hence the PSBR falls.[6] If the authorities do nothing, this leads to a fall in the money supply and this reinforces the deflationary effect of fiscal policy. On the other hand, the authorities could decide to keep interest rates and the money supply constant by buying bonds from the non-bank private sector and, hence, giving cheques and replacing the cut in money balances due to tax receipts exceeding government expenditure. In this case there would be no additional deflationary effect from the monetary implications of financing the PSBR.

If we now introduce open economy aspects, the fall in aggregate demand leads to a fall in imports while the fall in interest rates leads to a capital outflow. If capital is highly mobile the latter outweighs the former effect and we have a deficit in the balance of payments and downward pressure on the exchange rate. (This is the Mundell–Fleming model see Artis 1984, Cuthbertson and Taylor 1987.) Depreciation leads to expenditure switching and a tendency for net trade (exports less import volumes) to increase and hence aggregate demand to rise.

In summary, the primary impact on demand of a cut in government expenditure is negative via the usual Keynesian multiplier and positive via capital flows, the exchange rate and the expansion of net trade. In general, in the short run, the net effect on aggregate demand is negative and output falls. Finally, note that the effects on inflation are indeterminate in our qualitative analysis. A fall in aggregate demand puts downward pressure on wages and prices via the PEAPC, while the fall in the exchange rate has the converse effect. Only a complete econometric model can resolve this issue.

104   *The macroeconomy: a guide for business*

Rational expectations (RE) and policy

The assumption of rational expectations imply that private agents do
not make systematic errors when forecasting the future. This can have
strong implications for policy, for example, that systematic policy
rules do not influence output. However, it appears that as long as we
allow sluggish adjustment of prices and wages the addition of RE does
not radically alter the qualitative impact of monetary and fiscal policy
in 'real world' econometric models. However, the timing of the
response is usually speeded up with RE and there is a distinction
between anticipated and unanticipated changes in policy, as argued in
Chapter 2. We have already discussed these aspects in the case of
exchange rate overshooting resulting from monetary policy (see
Chapter 6). If changes are anticipated and an announced cut in the
money supply is believed, then prices may be altered at the time of the
announcement and before the actual cut in the money supply. Thus
the monetary policy effect is speeded up compared with a conventional
(i.e. non-RE) model where prices would not begin to change until
there was an actual change in the money supply.

Similar arguments apply to fiscal policy. With RE an anticipated
(announced) cut in government expenditure may result in changes in
aggregate demand prior to the actual change in government policy.
What is important here, even under RE, is the credibility of the
announcement. If the private sector thinks that the government may
renege on its announced policy when the time for government action
arises, then there may be no pre-emptive action by the private sector.
RE has yet to adequately model 'uncertainty' and the credibility
aspects of policy announcements. This argument is closely connected
with the time inconsistency of government policy: namely, it may pay
the government to renege on its announcement and this may, in fact,
be beneficial for the economy (see Sheffrin 1983 for a simple
exposition).

There is one final point that the businessman must remember when
interpreting forecasts that incorporate the actions of agents with
forward-looking behaviour. It is known as the Lucas critique. Lucas
(1976) argues that if the authorities (drastically) alter their policy
stance (regime), then the estimated coefficients in econometric equations may not be useful in forecasting under the new regime. This is
not a new idea. Forecasters have always recognized that agents'
behaviour might alter with changes in policy (for example, incomes
policy and the determination of wage inflation, to take an extreme
example), but Lucas's expostion was theoretically elegant, utilizing as

it did the then 'new' RE paradigm. To demonstrate Lucas's point as simply as possible, suppose we have a theory of the consumption function in our model, where consumption, C_t depends upon expected income, Y_t^e:

$$C_t^e = k Y_t^e \qquad (9.1)$$

Where Y_t^e is based on information available up to period t–1.

In addition, suppose that income has in the past grown at a (near) constant rate, g, because of a government policy of Keynesian fine tuning. Agents might then form a view of the next period's income, Y_t, according to:

$$Y_t^e = (1 + g) Y_{t-1} \qquad (9.2)$$

The estimated relationship in the model is then:

$$C_t = k(1 + g) Y_{t-1} \qquad (9.3)$$

If a new government comes to power and announces the end of 'demand management' (for example, the UK Conservative government of 1979), agents might (for example) expect income to remain constant:

$$Y_t^e = Y_{t-1} \qquad (9.4)$$

and hence the new consumption function is:

$$C_t = k Y_{t-1} \qquad (9.5)$$

Thus, if forecasters use the old consumption function (9.3) for forecasting they will overestimate consumption as (9.5) is now the 'true' relationship (and $k < k(1 + g)$).

The practical importance of the Lucas critique depends upon the severity of regime changes and their credibility. Forecasters by making residual adjustments, attempt to take acccount (admittedly in an *ad hoc* way) of 'minor' regime changes and announcements. In practice, the fact that many existing econometric relationships like (9.3) exhibit stable coefficients over time (Hendry 1983) provides some evidence that the practical importance of the Lucas critique may be overstated. It is only, perhaps, when modelling behaviour in money, bond and foreign exchange markets that the Lucas critique needs more careful consideration.

To sum up, we have now analysed the impact of monetary and fiscal policy on aggregate demand and some key business variables. We have also noted some implications of adding rational expectations to our analysis. However, we have merely been able to list the various transmission mechanisms (or causal routes) from the authorities' monetary and fiscal policy instruments to our main macroeconomic variables of interest. Valuable though this is in clarifying and interpreting published forecasts, we now move on to look at some illustrative quantitive results of the impact of policy changes using large-scale macroeconomic models of the United Kingdom.

9.2   POLICY SIMULATIONS

We now wish to look at the policy simulations of complete macroeconomic models of the United Kingdom to assess the impact of particular policy changes when all the interactions in the model are allowed for. In this way the businessman can interpret alternative forecasts of rival groups and also begin to understand the key factors in any model of the economy that he might have access to.

As we have seen, there are many rival models of the UK economy and each 'team' alters its model as new information (data) on the economy becomes available. It would, therefore, be extremely confusing if we gave a detailed analysis of all the UK models. Instead, for pedagogic reasons, we will be highly selective and concentrate on a particular version of the model used by HM Treasury in the early 1980s (Mowl 1980, Richardson 1981). By way of a summary, however, we also briefly compare these results with those from some other UK models. We will concentrate on the impact of changes in monetary and fiscal policy on our key business variables. We also briefly consider the impact of external disturbances, which may be defined as those not caused by changes in domestic policy.

Fiscal policy

The impact of an increase in government expenditure (equal to 0.5 per cent of GDP) on output and the price level is shown in Table 9.1 for accommodating and non-accommodating monetary policy, under a floating exchange rate.

Under an accommodating monetary policy, (i.e. money-financed deficit) the increase in the PSBR (i.e. broadly government expenditure less tax receipts) caused by an increase in government expenditure is financed by printing money (i.e. issuing cheques drawn on the Central Bank and payable to the NBPS) and interest rates are thereby held constant. The increase in government expenditure tends to increase real output (GDP) via the usual Keynesian multiplier process and this puts upward pressure on prices as unemployment falls and the wage-

Table 9.1 Increase in government expenditure of 0.5 per cent of GDP (in the base run) (HM Treasury model: floating exchange rate)

Assumptions	Money-financed deficit	Fixed money supply
% effect on output after		
3 months	0.4	0.4
2 years	0.7	0.4
4 years	0.7	0.1
% effect on prices after		
3 months	0.0	0.0
2 years	0.5	0.3
4 years	1.5	0.7

Source: Mowl (1980)

price mechanism of the Phillips curve gets under way. In this version of the Treasury model, FOREX dealers' expectations about the exchange rate are directly influenced by the growth in the money supply; the exchange rate for sterling is expected to fall as 'excess money' is thought to lead to additional purchases of foreign goods (i.e. trade flows) and foreign assets (i.e. capital flows). But if FOREX dealers waited for sterling to fall they would incur a loss and therefore they mark down sterling immediately. The fall in sterling tends to improve the price-competitive position of exports and to worsen it for imports, but the rise in import prices tends to reinforce the price–wage spiral (see section 8.1) and adversely affects competitiveness. In the short to medium term, however, the former outweighs the latter, price competitiveness improves and net trade (i.e. export minus import volume) expands and reinforces the positive fiscal multiplier effects.

The increase in the PSBR leads to an increase in the wealth of the private sector (initially in the form of the increased money balances of the recipients of increased government expenditure), but the rise in prices causes a fall in the purchasing power of money-fixed assets (such as cash, current accounts and possibly building society and bank deposit accounts). The latter is a revaluation of existing wealth and leads to additional saving, that is, lower consumers' expenditure, to rebuild the real value of money-fixed assets. Although this 'inflation loss' tends to reduce consumption, the other positive multiplier effects are dominant and the net effect on output is positive.

Prices are higher both because of higher import prices and higher output working via the Phillips curve (Table 9.1). Thus, in this macroeconometric model, there are a number of positive and negative feedbacks and the net effect of the policy change on, say, output depends upon the precise parameters (coefficients) of the behavioural equations. It is, therefore, understandable that models that appear broadly similar yield different multiplier effects and we illustrate this aspect below.

Turning now to the impact of the same increase in government expenditure under a fixed money supply (i.e. bond-financed deficit), the results are very different: output rises by much less than the initial increase in government expenditure (i.e. there is substantial crowding out) and prices also rise by less than in the previous simulation (Table 9.1). Why is this?

To keep the money supply constant, the authorities must finance the PSBR by selling bonds to the NBPS and this requires a rise in the interest rate on bonds to make them more attractive to investors. This leads to an increase in demand for sterling-denominated assets, a capital inflow and a rise in the sterling exchange rate (of 3 per cent in the effective exchange rate) by the fourth year.[7] Higher interest rates depress consumption, investment and stock building while the appreciation of sterling leads to a deterioration in price competitiveness and a fall in net trade. The fall in bond prices also leads to a fall in wealth and hence consumption. The net result is almost complete crowding out by the fourth year. Prices do not rise appreciably, partly because the increase in output is small (Phillips curve) and partly because the appreciation of sterling leads to lower sterling import prices and hence downward pressure on domestic prices.

Monetary policy

A 1 per cent reduction in the money supply by an open market sale of government bonds by the authorities to the NBPS requires a rise in interest rates. The latter has a direct deflationary impact on components of aggregate demand (for example, investment, consumption) and leads to a capital inflow and an appreciation of sterling. The latter causes net trade to fall slightly. In the first three years these effects depress the level of output, but in subsequent years the lower inflation caused by sterling appreciation reduces the inflation loss on money-fixed (liquid) assets, and consumers' expenditure and output increase slightly (Table 9.2). The eventual fall in the price level of 1 per cent demonstrates the neutrality property of this model (i.e. $\Delta m = \Delta p$) although the time lag involved is over nine years.

Table 9.2 Effect of a 1 per cent reduction in the money supply (£M3) by open market operations (HM Treasury model: flexible exchange rates[1])

Time period (years)	Output (GDP)	Price level GDP, deflator	Exchange rate[2] (effective)
1	−0.1	−0.1	1.1
3	−0.1	−0.4	0.8
5	0.0	−0.6	0.6
7	0.1	−0.7	0.4
9	0.2	−0.8	−0.2

Source: Richardson (1981)

Notes:
1 Figures are percentage differences from the 'base run'.
2 Positive values indicate an appreciation of sterling.

Comparison of fiscal simulations across different models

These may be illustrated by considering the government expenditure multipliers[8] under floating rates and a fixed money supply (i.e. bond financing) in Figure 9.1 for the London Business School (LBS), National Institute (NIESR) and HM Treasury models (as reported in Wallis *et al.* 1985).

The first point to note is the wide disparity in the value of the multipliers after about three years. This vintage of the HM Treasury model continues to exhibit (more than) complete crowding out (after four years) while the NIESR and LBS models have small but positive multipliers.

The second point to note is the difference in the NIESR multipliers when M1 (i.e. cash plus chequing accounts) rather than M3 (which includes a substantial amount of interest-bearing deposits) is the targetted monetary aggregate. The multiplier is smaller in the latter case because, in order to reduce the growth in sterling M3 (the broad money supply), we require a rise in interest rates on government bonds relative to those on 'money' (i.e. wholesale deposits). To increase this interest differential, the authorities have to raise the absolute level of interest rates by a substantial amount. A large rise in the absolute level of interest rates then has a large negative impact on interest-elastic expenditures (for example, investment and stock building) and via the exchange rate on net trade flows.

In contrast, the demand for narrow money, M1, depends only upon the absolute level of the interest rate on bonds (in fact, on local authority bills). Thus, a rise in absolute rates reduces M1 by a

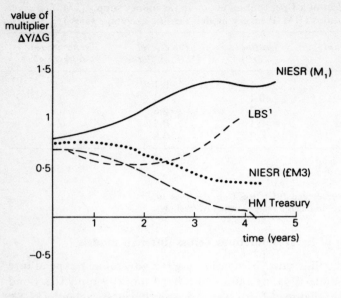

Figure 9.1 Government expenditure multipliers in alternative models: fixed money target
Note: 1 adaptive expectations used in the model

substantial amount. To control M1 therefore requires a smaller rise in the absolute level of interest rates than to control £M3 and this has a correspondingly smaller negative impact on aggregate demand.

The possible reasons for the different multipliers found in different models are given in Chapter 4, but the relative importance of each factor requires a detailed and complex analysis that we do not pursue here (see Brooks and Cuthbertson 1981, Wallis *et al.* 1985)

Other disturbances

Clearly, there are also non-policy disturbances that concern the businessman and that can be analysed in the same way. An important one referred to earlier is an oil price rise and it is, therefore, worth briefly considering this factor. In terms of the theoretical models outlined in Chapter 2, the effect of a rise in oil prices is to shift the supply curve to the left suggesting a short-run rise in prices and a fall in output. In the long run both these effects could be mitigated by compensating reductions in non-oil costs such as wages if workers adjusted their wage claims downwards in the face of the reduced

Table 9.3 Effect of a 10 per cent increase in world oil prices

% effect on output (GDP)	LBS	NIESR
Year 1	−0.1	—
2	−0.1	−0.1
3	−0.1	−0.2
4	−0.2	−0.2
5	—	−0.1
% effect on prices		
Year 1	—	—
2	−1.1	−0.3
3	−2.4	−0.5
4	−4.4	−0.7
5	—	−0.9

Source: Wallis *et al.* (1984)

potential output of the economy. What then of the models? In Table 9.3 we document the impact of a 10 per cent rise in world oil prices for the National Institute and London Business School models, on output and prices (a comparable simulation for HM Treasury is not readily available). For both models the output effects are similar and negative while, somewhat paradoxically, the price level falls in both models. It is worth noting that, although the effects here appear small, changes in oil prices can be very much larger than 10 per cent with a correspond-ing increased impact upon the United Kingdom economy. Domestic prices fall primarily because the rise in the value of domestic oil reserves has a direct positive impact upon the sterling exchange rate because of favourable expectations in the FOREX market. This appreciation outweighs the direct impact of the higher foreign currency (i.e. dollar) price of oil on sterling import prices. In addition, the appreciation of sterling reduces competitiveness and the conse-quent fall in net trade outweighs the positive stimulus to consumption resulting from a lower inflation loss on liquid assets. Hence output falls.

Clearly, the lessons from the above for the businessman are that the results of policy simulations may vary a great deal, both across models and according to the ancillary assumptions made (for example, fixed interest or exchange rates or fixed money supply). It is, therefore, far from simple for him to interpret the precise impact of policy or other external disturbances. A careful scrutiny of the existing models is, therefore, required. This has now become much easier (and cheaper) as 'user-friendly' versions of a number of UK macroeconometric models are now available for IBM-compatible machines.[9] As argued in Chapter 4, the businessman can therefore assess the sensitivity of published forecasts to his alternative chosen policy scenarios.

9.3   UK MACROECONOMIC POLICY AND THE EUROPEAN MONETARY SYSTEM (EMS)

From 1992, trade barriers and barriers to the free mobility of labour and capital within the twelve member states of the EC should be substantially removed. In addition, no national government should now be allowed to give subsidies that involve an unfair competitive advantage. There should be a level playing field, which will ensure free and fair competition in goods and financial services such as banking and insurance. Ten member states are, at present, members of the exchange rate mechanism (ERM) whereby governments pledge to keep their bilateral exchange rates within fixed bands (the narrow band is ± 2.25 per cent and the wider band is ± 6 per cent around the announced central rates). The entry of the UK into the ERM in October 1990 at a central rate against the Deutschmark (DM) of 2.95 DM/£ with a wide band of ± 6 per cent and the possible future adoption of a single European currency raise major issues about the future conduct of macroeconomic policy and its impact on UK business.

Let us take the DM as the anchor currency of the ERM. Upon entry in October 1990, the underlying rates of traded goods price inflation in the UK and Germany were about 8 per cent and 3 per cent, respectively. Suppose the central rate of 2.95 (DM/£) is perceived as credible by FOREX dealers and UK workers and management. Then one implication arising from purchasing power parity (PPP) is that, unless UK wage inflation falls rapidly, UK products will be priced out of German markets and UK unemployment will rise. Entry into the ERM is viewed by some advocates as a clear signal to UK wage bargainers (and a much more forceful signal than the mumbo jumbo of monetary targets that are rarely achieved) that wage growth must fall in line with productivity increases. The obvious alternative to voluntary wage restraint is a rise in UK unemployment, which will (via the Phillips curve) eventually lead to a fall in wage inflation. At the time of writing, UK inflation has fallen rapidly as a result of rising UK unemployment (while inflation in Germany has risen). Hence the transition costs of UK entry into the ERM are therefore likely to be high (as they were for other countries such as France and Italy in the 1980s) for several years to come.

If capital flows across the FOREX markets are highly mobile, then uncovered interest parity (UIP) should hold. When the UK entered the ERM, domestic interest rates were around 14 per cent while German interest rates were around 8 per cent. If UIP holds, this implies that FOREX dealers expect a depreciation of sterling against the DM of around 6 per cent – the lower limit of the UK's ERM band. However, since October 1990 UK interest rates have fallen yet sterling has remained within about ± 2 per cent of its central rate. Clearly, if the ERM is a credible policy, then UIP implies that UK rates should fall towards German rates and from then on will follow movements in German rates. Although there has been downward pressure on sterling from time to time, interest rates are now (summer 1992) broadly in line with those in Germany and should continue to be so, as the UK government continues to make clear that it will not tolerate a devaluation of sterling and as UK inflation falls towards that in Germany.

There is quite strong evidence that ERM countries (most of which joined the ERM at its inception in 1979) have experienced lower variability in bilateral nominal and real exchange-rates (i.e. price competitiveness) since joining (and particularly after the 1979–83 period). One might conjecture that this would involve a cost in terms of greater interest-rate volatility, as member states manipulate their interest rates to keep their exchange rates within the band. However, evidence also suggests that intra-ERM interest-rate volatility has also been reduced. This may be due to the fact that all ERM members agree to support each other's currencies in the FOREX market. So, for example, if the French franc comes under downward pressure against the DM, then both the Banque de France and the Bundesbank are obliged to step in and purchase francs (and unlimited funds are available for this under the so-called 'very short-term financing facility, VSTF). Thus the ERM system has now gained credibility and the volatility in interest and exchange rates has been reduced. To the extent that lower exchange- and interest-rate volatility encourages more trade in goods and services, cross-border investment and labour mobility, these dynamic real effects could provide long-term benefits to the members of the ERM. Thus, the ERM appears, once inflation and interest rates have converged, to reduce some of the uncertainties associated with the normal business decisions of pricing, borrowing costs and investment decisions within the EC countries.

The costs to the UK of entry include:

1 any induced increase in unemployment in order that inflation converges to the lower German rate; and
2 the inability of the UK authorities independently to alter their interest rate (i.e. monetary policy) or the exchange rate in order to influence the domestic economy.

There is, of course, some scope for independent changes in these macroeconomic policy variables within the ERM, as the band allows some flexibility. It is possible under the ERM rules to devalue – although the latter possibility, if repeated, would seem to defeat the whole counter-inflation strategy that underlies membership of the ERM.

If the ERM does lead to a convergence of inflation and interest rates, and less volatility in exchange rates, then a natural question to ask is whether it is worth going further and adopting a single currency across the EC to be used as the sole means of exchange. The momentum for this arose from the Delors Report of 1988, drawn up by the then president of the EC Commission, Jacques Delors, who first set out possible routes to full monetary union. Recently a revised timetable for implementation was agreed at the Maastricht summit of December 1991, details of which are given below. It should be noted that irrevocably fixed exchange rates and a single currency are very similar from the point of view of their implications for macroeconomic policy. Under both regimes governments do not have an independent monetary policy (interest rates across countries are equalized via UIP) or the ability to devalue. The added advantage of a single currency is that it saves on transactions costs, both pecuniary (i.e. financial costs in changing money) and the time, effort and resources involved in monitoring movements in individual EC currencies when determining financial portfolio, pricing and real investment decisions. (The European Commission has estimated financial cost savings from adopting a common currency at about 1.5 per cent of EC GDP.) With a single currency, member states effectively enter a monetary 'United States of Europe', with a 'Eurofed' Central Bank, which sets the single Euro interest rate, payable in terms of the single currency. (The latter is likely to be called the ECU, but this is not the function of the 'official ECU', which is used at present as a mere accounting device between central governments and in presenting some European firms' accounts.) Thus, the UK would become much like the state of Texas in the USA, namely, a region of this new common currency area.

If one is a monetarist, then the inflation rate throughout the whole EC will be set by the monetary policy of the Eurofed and monetary sovereignty of the UK Bank of England is lost. Interest-rate changes and hence any impact upon the UK domestic economy is determined by the Eurofed, not by the Bank of England and the UK Chancellor. Clearly, sovereignty over monetary policy is pooled in the constitutional set-up of the Eurofed – which is, at present, unknown (e.g. a simple example would be where each Central Banker has one vote and majority voting applies to all decisions). We have noted that interest rates do have an impact on the real economy and hence on unemployment, and the UK government will have no immediate direct control over this Euro interest rate.

Clearly, with a common currency one also loses the ability to devalue and improve ones' competitive position (e.g. Texas cannot devalue relative to Oklahoma in the US). However, it is arguable that devaluation only gives a very short-lived competitive advantage, as higher import prices lead to a domestic wage–price spiral and any initial competitive advantage is quickly eroded, say, over three years (see Chapter 7).

Fiscal policy (i.e. change in government expenditures, unemployment benefits and tax rates) in principle remains a viable option for individual member states to influence aggregate demand and unemployment (e.g. the state of Texas has it own budgetary powers). However, individual states may have to be constrained in their fiscal stance over a run of years. Individual Euro-states in the common currency area cannot finance their fiscal deficits by printing money (as this is to be determined by the Eurofed) and must therfore sell their own bonds (e.g. the state of New York issues its own bonds to finance additional spending). The interest rate on the bonds will, of course, be in terms of the single currency. However, interest rates on the bonds of profligate states may be higher than in states that adopt a prudent fiscal policy, in order to reflect the higher possible default risk. Even so, a relatively large element of fiscal autonomy could remain with individual countries even under a single currency. Perhaps surprisingly, there is little mention of fiscal issues in the Delors Report to guide one in this area.

If a series of regional problems develop within the EC (e.g. high unemployment in the UK or in a region of the UK), then the only options are labour or firm 'migration' or fiscal transfers. Unlike the USA, language problems will hinder labour migration from high to low unemployment countries. Nationalistic tensions could arise in areas of high unemployment where some 'immigrant workers' have jobs. An alternative to workers moving to the work is firms moving to the (unemployed) workers. To some extent this should happen automatically if real wage costs are low and other economic conditions (e.g. transport links and other infrastructure) are favourable in the high unemployment area. Note that free labour mobility is already accepted within the EC (by 1992) so what is important here are any additional costs and benefits in this area due to the adoption of a common currency. The Delors Report recognizes the possibility of increasing the Community budget devoted to regional aid to facilitate such structural changes, as the movement of workers or firms is likely to take many years.

9.4   EMU: AFTER MAASTRICHT

The Maastricht summit of December 1991 formulated a draft treaty for the movement towards a single currency (i.e. a so-called currency union) and also agreed a number of other matters of foreign policy and labour law. In what follows we shall be concerned only with those aspects that arise from the adoption of a common currency.

The procedure for moving to a single currency will begin in 1996. Finance ministers will at that point decide (by qualified majority voting) which member countries meet the so-called convergence criteria. If at least seven countries meet these criteria they will then decide when the common currency should start. If there is not the required critical mass of countries that meet the convergence criteria, then there will be another summit before July 1998 to decide, again by qualified majority voting, which members are ready to move to a common currency. At this point, a minimum of two member states could form a common currency area if they met the convergence criteria and a subset of countries will decide whether to move to a single currency in January 1999. The single currency will be known as the ECU and monetary policy will be in the hands of a single independent Central Bank (the Eurofed) with a commitment to maintain price stability.

The convergence criteria are as follows:

1 *Price stability*: No country participating in the common currency should have an inflation rate greater than 1.5 per cent above the average of the three EC countries with the lowest price rises.
2 *Interest Rates*: A similar convergence criterion applies to long-term interest rates, but the band this time is no more than two percentage points above the average of the three lowest interest rates.
3 *Fiscal deficits*: National budget deficits must be less than 3 per cent of GDP.

4 *Public debt*: The ratio of the stock of outstanding public debt (for example, primarily outstanding Treasury bills and gilt-edged stock in the UK) must not exceed 60 per cent of GDP.
5 *Currency stability*: A national currency must have been within the normal 2.25 per cent fluctuation margins of the ERM and must not have been devalued in the previous two years, in the run-up to the common currency period.

In Table 9.4 below we can see that, on the basis of these criteria, even Germany would not automatically qualify for full participation in the common currency and at present only France and Luxembourg satisfy all five criteria. It is also the case that the UK has obtained a legally binding protocol attached to the treaty, which allows it to decide whether to 'opt-in' to the common currency even if it fulfills the convergence criteria by 1996. It is likely that, come 1996–7, there will be some leeway over these criteria as they appear to be merely guidelines as to who must be allowed to enter the common currency area.

In view of our discussion above, the convergence criteria on price, interest rate and currency stability are highly like to be met by seven of the countries by 1996. These criteria are also eminently sensible on economic grounds. As argued above, an element of price stability is required if the entry costs to EMU in terms of higher unemployment are not to be excessively severe. However, the convergence criteria on the debt ratio seem restrictive and not strongly linked to broadly based economic ideas. From Table 9.4 one can see that the public debt to GDP ratio is exceedingly high for Denmark, Belgium, Ireland, Holland, Italy, Greece and Portugal. However, such a ratio bears little relation to the probability of a country successfully participating in a common currency area. A high outstanding stock of debt implies a commitment in the form of annual interest payments on the debt. In the extreme these interest payments can be financed by issuing even more debt to members of the non-bank private sector. However, this policy is clearly not sustainable in the long run. What is important is whether, over a run of years, governments can raise additional taxation (without undue real economic costs in terms of lost output) in order to finance such interest payments. Thus what seems of greater importance is the position of the budget deficit over a number of years and not the stock of outstanding debt. If the budget deficit can be brought into balance over a run of years, then the stock of public debt to GDP will not rise. A more sensible fiscal convergence criterion would therefore be to ensure that the budget deficits of all participat-

Table 9.4 Convergence criteria

| | Convergence indicators | | | Criteria satisfied? | | | | | |
| | Inflation rate | Long-term govt. bonds | Budget deficit | Public debt | Inflation rate | Long-term govt. bonds | Budget deficit | Public debt | Currency | Score |
	latest, %		1991 est., % of GDP							
France	2.5	8.8	-1.5	47	yes	yes	yes	yes	yes	5
Luxembourg	2.4	8.1	+2.0	7	yes	yes	yes	yes	yes	5
Denmark	1.8	8.8	-1.7	67	yes	yes	yes	no	no	4
Britain	3.7	9.7	-1.9	44	yes	yes	yes	yes	no	4
Germany	4.1	8.1	-3.6	46	no	yes	no	yes	yes	3
Belgium	2.8	8.9	-6.4	129	yes	yes	no	no	yes	3
Ireland	3.5	9.3	-4.1	103	yes	yes	no	no	yes	3
Holland	4.8	8.6	-4.4	78	no	yes	no	no	yes	2
Italy	6.2	12.6	-9.9	101	no	no	no	no	yes	1
Spain	5.5	11.7	-3.9	46	no	no	no	yes	no	1
Greece	17.6	20.8	-17.9	96	no	no	no	no	no	0
Portugal	9.8	14.1	-5.4	65	no	no	no	no	no	0

Sources: *National statistics*: JP Morgan: European Commission; The Economist, 14 December 1991, p. 56

ing countries should average zero over a run of years. It therefore makes sense to set a convergence criterion for the budget deficits of the various countries although the figure of 3 per cent in any particular year seems somewhat restrictive. This is because the budget deficit varies considerably over the economic cycle. In times of economic boom tax receipts rise faster than government expenditure and governments tend to be in surplus. In contrast, during a recession tax receipts are lower, unemployment benefits are higher and the government's budget is generally in deficit. Hence the need for a target for the budget deficit over a run of years with sufficient flexibility that individual countries can initiate some counter-cyclical fiscal policy. The latter, of course, assumes that fiscal policy can influence output in the short and medium term (say one to seven years), a proposition accepted by Keynesians but denied by monetarists and rational expectations economists.

Let us now turn to regional policy. At Maastricht, the development of a fund to help to pay for environmental and transport projects, particularly in the poorer countries, became known as the proposal on cohesion. It is not yet clear how big such a cohesion fund will be and what criteria will be used for distributing funds. However, what is clear is that the Maastricht agreement does not transfer a large amount of fiscal resources to a central body (i.e. an EC Treasury), which can then be used by this central body for regional policy purposes. Of course, it is open to individual national governments to undertake their own fiscal transfers between regions as long as these do not breach the convergence criteria described above (and do not involve any 'unfair' subsidies that might jeopardize the move to the single market in 1992).

Our general conclusion is that our discussion of the basic principles of the move towards EMU have been sensibly incorporated in the agreement at Maastricht, except for the tight fiscal convergence criteria with respect to government fiscal deficits and the adoption of a debt–GDP target. It seems more sensible for the members of the common currency area to say that they will not guarantee each others' debts, but will allow national governments to run relatively large fiscal deficits in the downswing of the economic cycle and finance these (temporary) deficits by issuing bonds either dominated in their own currency (i.e. the ECU) or borrowed in foreign currency (i.e. dollars). Private agencies will then provide explicit credit ratings for the various countries using the ECU and this will be reflected in the higher (ECU) interest rates they have to pay on their debt.

There is one final aspect of the treaty that seems somewhat at variance with economic theory. The Eurofed will control the issue of the currency and the interest rate payable on that currency. However, at present it seems that the EC Council of Ministers will be responsible for formal exchange-rate agreements and whether to intervene, for example, to support the ECU against the dollar or the yen in the FOREX market. However, as we have seen above and throughout much of this book, monetary policy and exchange-rate policy are indivisible. If the Eurofed decides that, in order to pursue price stability, it needs to raise the interest rate (payable in the common currency) this has obvious implications for the exchange rate of the ECU versus outside currencies such as the yen and the dollar. In general, the rise in ECU interest rates will tend to strengthen the ECU against the dollar and the yen. If the Council of Ministers feels that the exchange-rate implications of the interest-rate policy are unacceptable, then there is an obvious conflict between the Eurofed and the Council of Ministers. It would seem sensible if the Eurofed were given charge not only of interest-rate policy but of the exchange-rate policy that then ensues.

9.5   CONCLUSIONS

Economists have only recently begun to examine the issues surrounding currency union in Europe in any depth, and any calculation of possible costs and benefits of a single currency are highly speculative. However, casual empiricism suggests that businessmen feel that quasi-fixed exchange rates and the move to a single currency would be good for business. Presumably, besides the direct savings in changing and managing a portfolio of currencies, they believe the disappearance of two major uncertainties within Europe, namely numerous bilateral exchange rates and interest rates, will facilitate greater investment opportunities and allow more managerial resources to be devoted to production, location, marketing and design of products and services. However, this remains an open question on which we have little hard evidence.

Finally, note that the adoption of a single currency within the EC member states still leaves businessmen with all the problems associated with changes in the exchange rate of the European currency against the US dollar, yen and other currencies outside the EC: issues that we have analysed in earlier chapters.

In summary, we note that the disadvantages of entry into the ERM and the adoption of a single currency are straightforward: less direct control by the UK over interest rates and the loss of devaluation as a policy instrument. The potential advantages are not open to precise quantification but would include:

1 lower inflation and less uncertainty over exchange rates and interest-rate movements among the EC countries, both of which might lead to greater cross-border direct investment;
2 a more efficient allocation of capital and labour; and
3 savings in time and money (i.e. transactions costs) due to the removal of multiple currencies. Additional costs might involve more acute regional problems and some restrictions on the long-term fiscal deficits of individual countries. Whatever the economic arguments, the momentum for further European convergence and a move to a single currency seems, at present, to be inexorable. But we feel it is a strategy that businessmen on the whole support; presumably they regard it as high risk, but with high expected returns.

NOTES

1 The real rate of interest is equal to the nominal (market) rate *less* the expected rate of inflation (of investment goods prices). Use of this variable in determining real investment decisions assumes there exists a second-hand market in capital equipment so that nominal interest payments are offset by any rise in the second-hand price of the equipment. For example, leasing capital equipment is a method of reducing the risk attached to future inflation since the leasing contract is usually of a short duration and nominal interest costs are kept in line with inflation as the contract is renegotiated. The leasing company (usually a subsidiary of a large bank) then bears this 'inflation risk' rather than the firm.
2 See note 3, Chapter 8.
3 The simplest case here is the quantity theory approach. We have $M^d = kPY$ where M^d = demand for money, P = aggregate price level, Y = real income (transactions). For the money market to be equilibrium $M^s = kPY$ and with Y fixed at the 'natural' (full employment) rate in the long run, it follows that M^s is proportional to P. If the demand for money function also depends on the interest rate, this result still holds as long as there are no 'wealth effects' on the supply or demand for labour (see Cuthbertson and Taylor 1987 for further details).
4 This view is not held by new-classical economists who believe in rational expectations and that all 'prices' are flexible. Lags here are assumed to be very short.
5 We ignore any 'wealth effects' of a change in government bond holdings by the NBPS on consumption and investment expenditure, in what follows (see Cuthbertson and Taylor 1987 for further details).
6 The fall in income is $\Delta Y = h\Delta G$, where h = multiplier = $1/[1 - c_y(1 - t)]$, c_y = marginal propensity to consume, t_y = income tax rate. The change in tax receipts is $\Delta T = t_y \Delta Y = t_y h \Delta G$, and the change in the PSBR is

$\Delta G - \Delta T = \Delta G(1 - t_y h)$. It is easy to show that $(1 - t_y h) > 0$ and hence the PSBR falls when G falls.

7 The effective rate is a weighted average of the bilateral exchange rates between sterling and its major competitors.

8 The government expenditure (or fiscal) multiplier is the ratio of the change in (real) output to the change in real government expenditure.

9 The London Business School model is available from EFU, London Business School, Sussex Place, Regent's Park, London NW1 and the NIESR model from National Institute of Economic and Social Research, 2 Dean Trench Street, Smith Square, London SW1.

10 The role of policy

In the previous chapter, frequent mention has been made of policy as an important influence on the financial and international environments, and in the determination of prices and output levels. It therefore seems appropriate to examine the role of policy in some detail, for policy decisions will greatly affect the individual businessman. He will, therefore, wish to be aware of the main policy controversies, particularly as the policy arena is perhaps the one important one where the businessman can, through various channels, affect the policy formulation process. In the United Kingdom the various channels include, of course, the political parties, the Confederation of British Industry, the Institute of Directors, the National Economic Development Office and the professional organizations representing particular industries and/or skills. Other countries have similar bodies.

In assessing the role of policy it is, of course, important to bear in mind the policy aims. Sometimes these may conflict with one another as, for example, in the case of low unemployment and low inflation, or they may differ in the short and long run. An individual government may, for example, be more interested in winning an election at a certain time than in worrying about the long-term performance of the economy should it get re-elected. It follows, therefore, that we need to decide on a standard by which the businessman would want to judge economic policy at the macroeconomic level. A 'healthy economy' would be a reasonable criterion as evidenced by a high and consistent rate of output growth, low inflation and high unemployment.

In what follows, we begin with a wide perspective in examining the general case for intervention versus non-intervention before turning to detailed consideration of different levels of intervention and different types of interventionist approach.

10.1   INTERVENTION VERSUS NON-INTERVENTION

The debate on the extent to which governments should interfere in the running of economies has been revived in recent years as recession in the 1970s became partly identified with excessive intervention in many developed countries. The result has been a significant shift to the right and in many countries an increased reliance on market forces. It must be stressed that we are only talking in relative terms, for all governments need to interfere to some exent in providing, for example, defence and central banking. Moreover, governments are constrained by the fact that, in practice, most developed economies have a substantial public sector reflecting a less than complete reliance on the market mechanism. The argument is, then, whether economic prosperity is better achieved by decreasing or increasing government involvement.

The case for decreasing involvement is based on the views of the classical economists. Their views were founded on the doctrine of *laissez-faire* and they believed that the process of competition would serve society best. Market forces would ensure that only those businessmen who correctly anticipated the wants of consumers at a point in time would make profits, these being regarded as a desirable reward for enterprise. Given changes in preferences, changes in technology and continued competition, there was no need for government intervention. It was not needed to curb the excesses of the market, such as monopoly profits, because competition would ensure that they did not last. Moreover, it was not needed to pump-prime an economy as businessmen would be better able than government to take both a long- and a short-term view of profit-making opportunities.

The classic view of competition as a process has recently been revived with the increasing influence of Austrian economists such as Hayek. Such classicists argue that less government intervention and a return to *laissez-faire* are necessary to solve the fundamental weaknesses of western industry. The basis of their beliefs is that businessmen know best and in exercising their own self-interest they will be maximizing the welfare of society.

Monetarist and particularly neo-classical ideas are clearly in the classic tradition. In the monetarist case, the argument is that intervention should be limited to the keeping of simple rules of the type that the growth of the money supply should be pre-announced and based upon the government's inflation target. Monetarists argue against the Keynesian view that monetary and fiscal policy can be used to increase the stability of the business environment by smoothing out the booms and slumps that are otherwise endemic to the capitalist system. Indeed, monetarists argue that demand management may, in fact, be destabilizing with regard to the trade cycle. By the time the government has realized that the economy has gone into recession and has intervened to correct it, the economy would in all probability already be recovering. Thus government intervention would be likely to amplify the cycle by giving an added boost to the economy when it did not need it. The stop–go era of the 1950s and 1960s in the United Kingdom suggests some support for this view.

Neo-classical economists go even further by arguing that only unanticipated policy changes will have any impact, albeit a temporary one, on the real economy. However, such unanticipated changes should be avoided, as they tend to increase the variability of output while leaving the overall level of rate of growth unaffected.

Such ideas have gained widespread support in recent years in a number of Western countries including the United Kingdom, the USA, Germany and, more recently, France. They have led to the adoption of monetarist policies on the demand side of the economy while on the supply side encouragement has been given to privatization, to the abandonment of 'lame ducks' and to the promotion of new and small firms.

While the adoption of such policies may have revived some firms and even revitalized some economies, there is little evidence that they are a universal panacea. As far as the demand side of economic policy has been concerned, control of the money supply seems to have been a particularly illusive policy instrument – the uncontrollable in pursuit of the indefinable as one commentator caustically put it (Gilmour 1983). It now seems to have been effectively abandoned in the United Kingdom, in particular, as the sole indicator of the thrust of monetary policy.

In any event, evidence from a variety of developed countries would suggest that the free market does not provide the only solution to economic growth. Details of economic growth are given in Table 10.1 for a number of developed countries over the long term.

The fastest growing country has been Japan, where there has been close co-operation and planning between government and big business. Similarly, indicative planning operated in France and in Germany there has been close co-operation between banks and industry. Even in the USA, the bastion of free enterprise, much of the success of the whole economy and certainly of areas within it has been largely influenced by government defence procurement.

Table 10.1 Growth of real gross domestic product (GDP)

| | Average year-to-year percentage changes | | |
	1968–73	1973–9	1979–89
USA	3.2	2.4	2.8
Japan	8.7	3.6	4.1
Germany	4.9	2.3	1.8
France	5.4	2.8	2.1
UK	3.4	1.5	2.3
Italy	4.5	3.7	2.5
Canada	5.4	4.2	3.1

Source: OECD (1991) *Historical Statistics*

We should be wary of overcriticizing the classic case, however. There are cases where markets do not provide an optimal solution (for example, innovation and training) and also cases where the self-interest of the businessman does not square with the interests of the economy (for example, insider dealing). Equally, there are cases where public intervention (for example, some nationalization) has not been a great success and where increased competition would benefit the consumer.

Indeed, turning to the interventionist case, there are good and bad examples of policy. In most countries there has been a great deal of intervention to support declining industries, to support declining areas, to develop the wrong industries and to disguise unemployment. All this suggests that it is not so much intervention versus non-intervention that should be at issue, but rather the formulation of good as opposed to bad policy to complement the basic market system.

10.2 TYPES OF INTERVENTION

As for interventionist policies, these may broadly be split into those primarily affecting the supply side of an economy and those affecting the demand side.

Supply-side policies, which have become increasingly popular, include privatization and de-regulation. Early evidence for the UK suggests that, in many cases, efficiency has improved as a result. There is some doubt, however, as to whether the full gains have gone to the consumer for, in many cases, to make sell-offs attractive to investors monopoly positions have been maintained, at least for a particular time.

Longer-standing supply-side policies have included tripartite planning agreements between industry, trade unions and government, as operated in Scandanavia, Japan and France. The idea here is that economic growth is better fostered by an atmosphere of collaboration than confrontation, and it certainly did seem to be successful for long periods in the above cases. Other supply-side policies include subsidies and grants to particular industries.

In recent years, all governments have seen the need to promote the growth of micro-electronics, for example, and none has been prepared to leave this completely to market forces. Whether they should have done so or, alternatively, intervened to a greater extent is of some interest. Certainly, the European micro-electronics industry is in extreme difficulty at the time of writing and more than ready to submit to the take-over aspirations of Japanese firms.

Also in recent years, many grants and allowances have been directed at new entrepreneurs and existing small firms, and at training and retraining. Yet other policies have been directed at particularly underdeveloped, depressed or developing areas, such as the regional policy of the EC and various member states. A key supply-side policy in some countries is tax cuts for individuals and firms, the idea being to encourage an enterprise culture, innovation and productivity.

A final supply-side measure is incomes policy. The idea here, as argued in Chapter 2 (Figure 2.9), is to enable demand-side policies to ensure an appropriate supply-side response. Although new incomes policies of the tax-based variety are still advocated in some quarters (Layard 1986), past policies do not appear to have been very successful in the United Kingdom – except in the short run.

This brings us to the demand side and in particular, to monetary and fiscal policy, which we have already examined in some detail. It might be argued that demand-side policy of some kind is necessary to provide an environment conducive to business optimism. Keynesians, in particular, would argue that although supply-side considerations are important they are not on their own sufficient to encourage businessmen to undertake investment in a period of recession. An example is provided by wage cuts, given that these are frequently suggested by monetarists as a cure to unemployment. But wage cuts on their own are likely to depress aggregate demand and why should firms take on more labour or, indeed, expand output when sales are falling? All this suggests that demand considerations do not and should not operate independently of supply. As for which type of demand-side policy, there are, as suggested above, interdependencies between monetary and fiscal policy, and in the USA the Reagan administration used both simultaneously. Indeed, perhaps more controversy is attached to which type of fiscal or monetary policy. As far as monetary policy is concerned, there has been little success in controlling the broad monetary aggregates and reliance is now back on a 'look at everything' approach in the monetary field.

In the UK, entry into the exchange rate mechanism (ERM) means that maintaining the value of the pound is of particular importance in the counter-inflation strategy. As far as fiscal policy is concerned, there is the question of whether increased public expenditure or tax cuts are the best method of reflating an economy. Those in favour of tax cuts stress that the individual should decide where to spend his money and that incentive effects are important, while those in favour of public expenditure argue that much of the benefit of tax cuts in highly open economies such as the United Kingdom is likely to leak into imports. Thus tax cuts have both a supply-side (i.e. incentive effect) and a demand-side effect.

Other possible demand-side measures include the restriction of imports and the encouragement of exports, although risks of retaliation can be significant and there is now a general trend to removing import restrictions via the GATT negotiations, the opening up of Eastern Europe and the removal of trade barriers within the EC by 1992.

To sum up, we have only outlined the various controversies regarding the role of economic policy and it would be possible to write a book on these issues alone. The businessman will clearly have his own views on which type of policy is most appropriate, both for a country generally and for his industry or firm in particular. We hope, however, that this book has helped him to take an informed position and that, therefore, he will be effective in making his voice heard both within his own firm and in the wider public domain.

11 Overview

We have now concluded our examination of the major macroeconomic influences affecting business. We finish by drawing together some of the important points made in previous chapters.

We begin by restating that the business environment is constantly changing and firms must adapt to survive. At one time the theoretical literature of both micro and industrial economics was largely about firms reacting passively to the environment and, particularly, the market structure that they faced. It is now increasingly recognized that successful firms engage in active behaviour both to understand and to mould that environment. To do so, they require a strategy to reduce the level of uncertainty, to reduce the impact of change and to achieve the targets they set themselves. This applies in the long run, an area that is normally covered by courses in business policy, and also to short-run decisions in the so-called functional areas of finance, marketing, production and the management of labour resources. It is, therefore, clearly important that both businessmen and business students understand the importance of the operating environment and the effect it can have on business decisions.

There are, of course, many influences that affect business and we have focused on the macroeconomic ones. In doing so, we have attempted in most cases to lay down general principles, which can be applied across a wide spectrum of business, rather than to present a case-study approach. The reason, of course, is that every business is unique and so are many business problems. We can only hope that the reader is now better equipped to understand the importance of changes in the macroeconomy and how to allow for them.

The first point we have emphasized in this respect is that businessmen should be aware of the information available on the macroeconomy and should be able both to use and interpret it. This applies both to past and present data and to the use of forecasts. As we argued in Chapter 4, this can be done with various degrees of sophistication and the day is fast approaching when businessmen can produce their own forecasts on personal computers or conduct sensitivity analyses on somebody else's macroeconomic model at relatively low cost. The usefulness of economic forecasts is suggested by the fact that private companies are major clients of the various forecasting bodies and, indeed, in some cases (such as the London Business School) are important financiers of the forecasting team.

The second point is that businessmen need to be aware of the international aspects of business, particularly if they operate in an economy as open as that of the United Kingdom. We have examined issues such as the use of hedging, portfolio diversification and the forward market to avoid exchange-rate risk. We have also looked at longer-term measures for diversifying foreign assets, such as the establishment of foreign subsidiaries. These are important aspects of modern business.

An interesting example of a firm that failed partly because of exchange-rate factors was Laker Airways, which folded in 1982. Although recession in the airline industry, high interest rates and a very high debt to equity ratio were also important, Laker's problems were compounded by the fact that some of the borrowing was in the USA and had to be repaid in dollars. The weakening of the sterling–dollar exchange rate, and the fact that much of the firms' income was presumably in sterling, 'wreaked havoc' with its 1981–2 budget (Donne and Friedman 1982). The Laker case demonstrates the interaction between exchange rates and capital markets, a topic that we have examined in some detail. Clearly, businessmen need to be aware of the importance of international interest rates and of the financial policies of domestic and foreign governments.

The third point, then, concerns awareness and relates to both international and domestic capital markets. One aspect of this is that the cost of capital to a firm depends upon the mix of finance chosen, which in turn depends upon a whole set of interest rates, from those on bank loans to those on bonds and equity. Foreign rates also play a part as firms increasingly seek funds in Euromarkets. The entry of the UK into the ERM and the possible adoption of a single European currency will considerably alter the market environment faced by business.

It is, of course, important for firms to diversify their domestic as well as their foreign assets. The case of London and Counties Securities is illustrative in this respect. This secondary bank borrowed money on the London money markets which it then invested very largely in 'illiquid' property during the property boom of the early 1970s. The problem was that the company borrowed 'short' and lent 'long' so that, when short-term interest rates rose, its profits were squeezed. In addition, the end of the property boom made its assets less valuable and depositors began to lose confidence. There was a run on deposits and the Bank of England had to step in to rescue the bank and to prevent a crisis of confidence in the banking system as a whole. Unfortunately, the lessons were not entirely learnt. The boom in the 1980s led to extensive property speculation in many parts of the developed world. The onset of recession at the end of the decade caused a slump in property values and many property companies in the UK, in particular, went bankrupt. As a result, bank profits fell significantly.

Our fourth point concerns inflation and its effect on the planning of budgets. Inflation affects the costs of goods and labour and also future selling prices, so it is extremely important that businessmen allow for it in both the planning process and the negotiation of contracts. We have, therefore, examined in some detail both the theoretical determinants of price changes and also inflation forecasts.

Our final point is that businessmen need to know how policy changes are likely to affect them. In the short run, we have emphasized that this is a matter of how best to adapt to policy announcements, given their likely impact on the major economic variables such as exchange rates, interest rates, and wages and prices. In the long run, it is a question of how businessmen can understand and contribute to the debates essential to the formulation of policies affecting the economic environment in which they operate.

Self-assessment questions

2 ECONOMIC FOUNDATIONS

1 'It's about time economists got their act together.' Discuss.
2 'Economics is a positive science in which hypotheses are put forward, tested and accepted or refuted. As a result, our knowledge of how the economy works is improving all the time.' Discuss.
3 Why does the aggregate demand curve slope downwards? What will make the curve shift to the left?
4 'There is little controversy about aggregate demand; all the arguments are about aggregate supply.' Discuss.
5 How is the long run defined in the analysis of aggregate supply?
6 What is meant by the proposition that money is neutral?
7 Why is the short-run aggregate supply curve upward sloping while the long-run aggregate supply curve is vertical? Do shifts in the aggregate supply curve depend solely upon technological innovation and productivity?
8 Explain the term 'rational expectations'
9 What factors determine whether an increase in aggregate demand will lead to an increase in prices or output?
10 What are the essential differences between:
   a) classical and neo-classical monetarists?
   b) monetarists and Keynesians?

3 RISK AND ITS IMPACT ON BUSINESS

1 What do you understand by the term business cycle? To what extent is it affected in any one country by:
   a) national government policy?
   b) international influences?
2 'It could be argued that macroeconomic events have more effect on a business than the quality of management.' Discuss.

3 Distinguish between the terms long-wave and short-wave when discussing economic cycles.
4 How are business cycles measured in the UK?
5 What has happened to the amplitude and duration of UK cycles in output since 1960? (Use data on GDP from *Economic Trends*, annual supplement.)
6 To what extent does the business cycle impinge upon business decisions?
7 How can firms deal with risk caused by changes in macroeconomic events?
8 Explain the following terms: coincident indicator, longer leading indicator, shorter leading indicator. How are they calculated?
9 How useful are leading indicators for business planning?
10 What do you understand by the term political business cycle? What evidence is there for its existence?

4 THE USE OF FORECASTS

1 Why are there so many agencies producing forecasts of the UK economy?
2 Why do economic forecasts differ?
3 Explain the following terms: behavioural equation, structural equation, residual, constant, exogenous and endogenous variable, 'add-on' factor.
4 To what extent and in what ways might forecasts using large-scale macroeconomic models be subject to judgemental elements?
5 Outline the main characteristics of any two UK forecasting models.
6 Why is it so difficult to rank economic forecasts?
7 'Forecasting is a bogus scientific exercise, the results of which, if used at all, should be used with great caution.' Discuss.
8 What are satellite economic models; how useful are they?
9 What do you understand by the term sensitivity analysis in the forecasting context?
10 a) Using data from *Economic Trends* and the *Society of Motor Manufacturers and Traders*, try to develop and defend a forecasting equation for UK sales of new cars in the 1980s.
   b) Using data for 1990 and 1991, use your forecasting equation to predict car sales for those years.
   c) Compare your forecasts with the actual figures; comment on and, if possible, explain the differences.
   d) Develop a satellite model for explaining the sales of any one UK manufacturer.

e) Suggest ways in which the models might be improved.
[Note: you will need knowledge of regression analysis and access to a computer regression package to do this question.]

5   THE INFLUENCE OF EXCHANGE RATES ON BUSINESS

1 'A firm selling a heterogeneous product has more discretion over the price it sets in foreign markets than one selling a homogeneous product.' Discuss.

2 What do you understand by the terms 'spot' and 'forward' rate? How are they presented in the financial press?

3 How can a firm seek to minimize exchange risk?

4 What is meant by hedging? When and how is it used in foreign-exchange dealings and transactions involving foreign currencies (assets)?

5 How far do operations in the forward (FOREX) market safeguard a business in ensuring the viability of a contract with foreign partners?

6 Explain the basic elements behind currency options and currency swaps.

7 Given that using the forward market reduces exchange-rate risk, why don't all importers and exporters use it?

8 Explain the difference between covered and uncovered interest (rate) parity.

9 How are forward rates calculated from spot rates given the information in the financial press? Calculate the $/£ exchange rate one month and three months forward in the following case:

Spot rate

Close	1 month: premium/discount	3 months: premium/discount
1.3075–1.3085	0.40–0.37 cents pm	1.03–0.98 cents pm

10 Your company has to make a US $0.5 million payment in one year's time. The dollars are available now. You decide to invest them for the year and are given the following information:

- the US deposit rate is 8 per cent per annum;
- the sterling deposit rate is 10 per cent per annum;
- the spot exchange rate is $1.70/£; and

- the three-month forward rate is $1.62/£
a) Where should your company invest for the better return?
b) Assuming that interest rates and spot exchange rates remain the same, what forward rate would yield a situation where one was indifferent as to whether one held pound or dollar deposits?
c) Assuming that the US dollar interest rate and the forward rates remain as above, where would you invest if the sterling deposit rate was 14 per cent per annum?
d) With the originally stated spot and forward rates, and the same dollar deposit rates, what is the value of the sterling deposit rate that would make you indifferent as to whether you held pound or dollar assets?

6   THE DETERMINATION OF EXCHANGE RATES

1 'Chartism, even sophisticated chartism, has no basis in rational behaviour and hence should be treated with care and avoided where possible.' Discuss.
2 What are resistance levels?
3 What is the purchasing power parity (PPP) theory of the relationship between prices and exchange-rate determination? Does it apply in practice over the short term or the long term?
4 'Evidence suggests that simple models for forecasting exchange rates perform as well as complex ones.' Discuss.
5 Why do exchange rates overshoot and why are they highly volatile?
6 What is a random walk model?
7 'Exchange rates are impossible to predict in the short run as they bear little relationship to economic fundamentals.' Discuss.
8 Explain the difference between:
a) single equation models
b) complete macroeconomic models in forecasting exchange rates.
9 How can 'rational expectations' help us to understand short-run changes in exchange rates?

7   THE FINANCIAL ENVIRONMENT

1 What do you understand by the term ripple effect? Demonstrate how it would operate if the government tried to increase the money supply by buying short-term commercial bills.
2 What is 'the term structure of interest rates'? How is it related to the 'yield' curve?
3 Why should a rise in interest rates cause a reduction in investment?

Would this still be true in a firm that financed all its investment out of retained earnings?

4 How would rational expectations on the part of speculators affect the response of interest rates to domestic and foreign government policy?

5 At 11 a.m. one day, the Federal Reserve Board announces a target reduction in the growth of the US money supply of 5 per cent for the next financial year. UK interest rates immediately rise by 1 per cent. Later in the day, an announcement is made about the discovery of new oil reserves in the North Sea and the interest rate drops by 0.5 per cent. Explain why this might happen. If, on the other hand, UK interest rates remained stable after the rise in US rates, why might this happen?

6 Interest rates on government bonds are 12 per cent in the UK and 10 per cent in the USA. Why might this be?

7 'The determination of interest rates is only partly explained by uncovered interest-rate parity.' Explain.

8 What is the efficient markets hypothesis? Does it apply in practice?

8   WAGES AND PRICES

1 Using the AD–AS model, explain how an increase in government spending financed by an expansion of the money supply will increase the rate of inflation. Will it affect output in the long run?

2 What is natural about the 'natural rate of output'?

3 What is the NAIRU? Can it be changed by government policy?

4 Discuss the economic and statistical merits of the following equation, based on time series data over forty quarters for a macroeconomy:

$$\Delta P_t = 2.86 + 0.5 \ \Delta p_{t-1} + 0.3 \ \Delta wt + 0.2 \ \Delta I_{t-1}$$
$$\quad\quad (2.1) \quad (1.4) \quad\quad (3.8) \quad\quad (2.4)$$

$R^2 = 0.69$

(.) = t-statistic

ΔP = rate of price inflation (per cent p.a.)

Δw = rate of wage inflation (per cent p.a.)

ΔI = rate of inflation in import costs (per cent p.a.)

t, t–1 and t–2 are time subscripts.

If wage inflation rises by 1 per cent p.a., what is the initial effect on price inflation and what is the effect in the long run? What might the intercept term 2.86 represent?

[Note: you will need some knowledge of regression analysis to do this question.]

5 What are the main causes of wage and price inflation? How can they be incorporated in a forecasting model for wage and price inflation, and how can these two equations be used to analyse the wage–price spiral?

9 MONETARY AND FISCAL POLICY AND THE EUROPEAN MONETARY SYSTEM

1 What are the main transmission mechanisms by which monetary and fiscal policy operate?
2 What is meant by the statement 'money is neutral'? How neutral is it in the HMT model?
3 In what circumstances could fiscal policy have a near-zero effect on output? How realistic do you think this scenario is?
4 If firms, workers, etc. have rational expectations, what implications does this have for the impact of fiscal and/or monetary policy?
5 What do you understand by the term Lucas critique? Is it likely to be important?
6 'The exchange rate mechanism (ERM) violates the principle that the price of currencies should be left to market forces and hence is bound to be inferior to freely floating exchange rates.' Discuss.
7 'UK acceptance of the ERM is an inevitable step to a single European currency and hence the handing over of all aspects of UK macroeconomic policy to a European Central Bank.' Discuss.

10 THE ROLE OF POLICY

1 To what extent should governments intervene in the running of an economy?
2 Consider the extent to which the performance of the UK economy benefited from Thatcherism.
3 'Privatization in the UK has done little more than substitute private for public monopoly.' Discuss.
4 Distinguish between demand- and supply-side interventionist policies. Give examples of each.
5 'It will be better for business if there is complete monetary union within the European Community.' Discuss.
6 Should Britain have entered the EMS?
7 Discuss the impact of the 'peace dividend' on the UK and its regions.

8 'The argument should not be about intervention or non-intervention. It should be about good or bad policy.' Discuss.
9 Evaluate the success of supply-side industrial policy as applied to training and/or innovation in any one country by comparing it with others.
10 A financier, an industrialist and a right-wing politician meet to discuss the future direction of economic policy. How do you think the discussion might have gone?

Further reading

Below we give a highly selective list of further reading on the topics covered in this text. Except where stated otherwise the references listed should provide a manageable increase in the degree of complexity of exposition.

CHAPTER 2

There is a plethora of introductory macroeconomics texts. Begg, Fischer and Dornbusch (1991), Parkin and Bade (1982) and Creedy *et al.* (1984) provide a nice balance between theory and recent historical narrative for the United Kingdom. Dornbusch and Fischer (1990) use primarily US examples. Crystal (1983) and Pratten (1990) also provide a succinct account and also link theory with 'real world' models of the United Kingdom economy, while Artis (1984) provides a useful, concise development of the main theoretical issues. Another useful applied reference for the UK is Griffiths and Wall (1991). A more advanced treatment can be found in Cuthbertson and Taylor (1987).

CHAPTER 3

Davis and Pointon (1984) and Lumby (1984) provide a clear, thorough introduction to investment appraisal, other financial decisions that face the firm and the problems of risk and uncertainty. Also useful are Begg, Fischer and Dornbusch (1991) and McKenna (1986).

Forecasts for the OECD countries are provided biannually in the OECD *Economic Outlook*, and the London Business School *Economic Outlook* and the *National Institute Economic Review* (both quarterly) also provide commentary on the world economy. A useful text on business strategy is Johnson and Scholes (1990).

CHAPTER 4

Useful books on macroeconomic forecasting include Wallis *et al.* (1987) and Keating (1985a). A wider treatment of business forecasting in general is given in Holden, Peel and Thompson (1990).

CHAPTER 5

The excellent book by Brett (1991) explains in simple but comprehensive terms details of foreign-exchange markets and the institutions and businesses operating in them. Cuthbertson (1979) provides a useful account of the behaviour of exports and imports and their interaction with the exchange rate. Brooks *et al.* (1986), Hallwood and MacDonald (1986) and Copeland (1989) deal with capital flows and the wider problems of international monetary arrangements.

A good book on multinational finance is Buckley (1990), while Grimwade (1989) gives details of recent patterns of international trade, production and investment.

CHAPTER 6

A compendium of papers on the exchange rate and monetary policy is to be found in Eltis and Sinclair (1981). Particularly accessible to the non-specialist are contributions by Worswick, Laidler, Dimsdale, Brech and Stout. Keating (1985a) discusses the problems in forecasting the exchange rate, while the papers by Beenstock *et al.* and Hacche and Townend in Eltis and Sinclair (1981), although more complex, provide useful examples of single equation econometric studies of the exchange rate. Dornbusch (1980) is a useful but fairly advanced theory text, while Copeland (1989) is an eminently readable theory text.

CHAPTER 7

Bain and Howells (1985) provide an introductory account of United Kingdom monetary policy, Dennis *et al.* (1982) give a detailed account of the institutional structure of the United Kingdom financial sector and Hall (1987) concentrates on financial innovation and deregulation. Llewellyn (1980) and Johnston (1983) focus on the international capital markets. A more advanced treatment of the demand for domestic and foreign assets can be found in Cuthbertson (1986) and insights into some wider issues are to be found in Goodhart (1984) and Laidler (1982). Artis and Lewis (1991) provide a readable, up-to-date account of UK monetary policy.

CHAPTER 8

Inflation is dealt with in all the introductory texts listed for Chapter 2, but a clear and concise exposition is also to be found in Flemming (1976). Useful surveys are Laidler and Parkin (1975) and Gordon (1976), while Friedman's (1968) seminal article is eminently readable. Dornbusch and Fischer (1990), and McNabb and McKenna (1989), also give a useful exposition of inflation.

CHAPTER 9

Pindyck and Rubinfeld (1976) is a useful blend of theory and application in model building and forecasting, although it requires some prior statistical knowledge. For an intuitive approach to estimation see Kennedy (1979). Sheffrin (1983), Carter and Maddock (1984), and Shaw (1984) give an introductory treatment of rational expectations. The main source for an account of United Kingdom models is Wallis *et al.* (1984 and 1985), but Morris (1985) and Curwen (1990) provide a simpler account of United Kingdom models and recent United Kingdom policy.

Useful commentary on the United Kingdom and world economies can be found in quarterly publications such as the *Bank of England Quarterly Bulletin,* the *National Institute Economic Review*, the London Business School *Economic Outlook* and the OECD *Economic Outlook*.

CHAPTER 10

A useful wide-ranging text is Hartley (1977), which discusses the case for and against intervention and various other aspects of policy. Grant and Shaw (1980) is also useful, as are Cross (1982) and Crystal (1983). See also Griffiths and Wall (1991) and Curwen (1990) for applied discussion in a UK context.

References

Allen, D. E. (1983) *Finance: A Theoretical Introduction*, Oxford: Blackwell.

Artis, M. (1984) *Macroeconomics,* Oxford: Oxford University Press.

Artis, M. and Lewis, M. K. (1991) *Money in Britain*, Philip Alan.

Bain K. and Howells, R. G. A. (1985) *Monetary Economics*, London: Longman.

Barr, D. G. and Cuthbertson, K. (1991) 'Neoclassical consumer demand theory and the demand for money', *Economic Journal*, July: 855–76.

Beenstock, M., Budd, A. and Warburton, P. (1981) 'Monetary policy, expectations and real exchange rate dynamics', in W. Eltis, and P. Sinclair (eds) *The Money Supply and the Exchange Rate*, Oxford: Oxford University Press.

Begg, D., Fischer, S. and Dornbusch, R. (1991) *Economics*, 3rd edn, New York: McGraw-Hill.

Brett, M. (1991) *How to Read the Financial Pages*, 3rd edn, Hutchinson.

Brooks, S. and Cuthbertson, K. (1981) 'Economic models and economic forecasts', *National Institute Economic Review* 95: 21–31.

Brooks, S., Cuthbertson, K. and Meyes, D. (1986) *The Exchange Rate Environment*, London: Croom Helm.

Buckley, A. (1990) *The Essence of International Money*, Prentice Hall.

Carter, M. and Maddock, R. (1984) *Rational Expectations: Macroeconomics for the 1980's?*, London: Macmillan.

Central Statistical Office (1991) *Economic Trends* 449.

Central Statistical Office (1991) *Economic Trends* 457.

Central Statistical Office (annual) *Financial Statistics*, London: HMSO.

Copeland, L. S. (1989) *Exchange Rates and International Finance*, Addison Wesley.

Creedy, J., Evans, L., Thomas, B., Johnson, P. and Wilson, R. (1984) *Economics: An Integrated Approach,* London: Prentice Hall.

Cross, R. (1982) *Economic Theory and Policy in the United Kingdom*, Oxford: Martin Robertson.

Crystal, K. A. (1983) *Controversies in Macroeconomics*, 2nd edn, Oxford: Philip Allan.

Curwen, P. (1990) *Understanding the UK Economy*, Macmillan.

Cuthbertson, K. (1979) *Macroeconomic Policy*, London: Macmillan.

Cuthbertson, K. (1980) 'The determination of expenditure on consumer durables', *National Institute Economic Review* 94: 62–72.

Cuthbertson, K. (1982) 'The measurement and behaviour of the United

Kingdom saving ratio in the 1970s', *National Institute Economic Review* 99: 75–84.

Cuthbertson, K. (1983) 'Consumer spending', in A. J. C. Britton (ed.) *Employment, Output and Inflation*, London: Heinemann.

Cuthbertson, K. (1984) 'Techniques of monetary control in the United Kingdom', *Journal of Economic Studies* 11 (4): 46–68.

Cuthbertson, K. (1986) *The Supply and Demand for Money*, Oxford: Blackwell.

Cuthbertson, K. and Taylor, M. P. (1987) *Macroeconomic Systems*, Oxford: Blackwell.

Davidson, J. E. H., Hendry, D. F., Srba, F. and Yeo. S. (1978) 'Econometric modelling of aggregate time series relationship between consumption and income in the United Kingdom', *Economic Journal* 88: 661–92.

Davis, E. W. and Pointon, J. (1984) *Finance and the Firm*, Oxford: Oxford University Press.

Delors, J. (1989) *Report on Economic and Monetary Union in the European Community*, Luxembourg: Office for Official Publications of the European Communities.

Dennis, G. E. J., Hall, M., Llewellyn, D. and Nellis, G. J. (1982) *The Framework of United Kingdom Monetary Policy*, London: Heinemann.

Donne, M. and Friedman, A. (1982) 'The fight Sir Freddie lost', *Financial Times*, 6 February.

Dornbusch, R. (1980) *Open Economy Macroeconomics*, New York: Basic Books.

Dornbusch, R. and Fischer, S. (1990) *Macroeconomics*, 5th edn, New York: McGraw-Hill.

Eltis, W. and Sinclair, P. J. N. (eds) (1981) *The Money Supply and the Exchange Rate*, Oxford: Oxford University Press.

Flemming, J. S. (1976) *Inflation*, Oxford: Oxford University Press.

Friedman, B. (1977) 'Financial flow variables and the short run determination of lend term interest rates', *Journal of Political Economy* 85 (4): 661–89.

Friedman, M. (1968) 'The role of monetary policy', *American Economic Review* 58: 1–17.

Gilmour, I. (1983) *Britain Can Work*, Oxford: Martin Robertson, 142.

Goodhart, C. A. E. (1984) *Monetary Theory and Monetary Practice: The United Kingdom Experience*, London: Macmillan.

Gordon, R. J. (1976) 'Recent developments in the theory of inflation and unemployment', *Journal of Monetary Economics* 2: 185–219.

Grant, R. M. and Shaw, G. K. (1980) *Current Issues in Economic Policy*, Oxford: Philip Allan.

Griffith, A. and Wall, S. (1991) *Applied Economics*, 4th edn, London: Longman.

Grimwade (1989) *International Trade*, London: Routledge.

Hall, M. (1987) *Financial Deregulation*, London: Macmillan.

Hall, S. G., Henry, S. G. B. and Wren Lewis, S. (1986) 'Manufacturing stocks and forward-looking expectations in the United Kingdom', *Economica* 53 (212): 447–66.

Hallwood, P. and MacDonald, R. (1986) *International Money*, Oxford: Blackwell.

Hartley, K. (1977) *Problems of Economic Policy*, London: Allen & Unwin.

144   *References*

Hendry, D. F. (1983) 'Econometric modelling: the "consumption function" in retrospect', *Scottish Journal of Political Economy* 30 (3): 193–220.

Hendry, D. F. and von Ungern-Sternberg, T. (1979) 'Liquidity and inflation effects on consumers' expenditure', in A. S. Deaton (ed.) *Essays in the Theory and Measurement of Consumers' Behaviour*, Cambridge: Cambridge University Press.

HM Treasury (1982) *Macroeconomic Model Technical Manual*, London: HM Treasury.

HM Treasury (1990) *Comparison of Outside Forecasts*, London: HM Treasury.

Holden, K., Peel, D. A. and Thompson, J. L. (1990) *Economic Forecasting: an Introduction*, Cambridge: Cambridge University Press.

Holly, S. and Longbottom, A. (1985) 'A model of company acquisitions and investment using Tobin's Q', *London Business School Discussion Paper* 142.

Johnson, G. and Scholes, K. (1990) *Exploring Corporate Strategy*, 2nd edn, London: Prentice Hall.

Johnston, R. B. (1983) *The Economics of the Euromarkets*, London: Macmillan.

Jorgenson, D. W. (1971) 'Econometric studies of investment behaviour: a survey', *Journal of Economic Literature*, 9: 1111–47.

Keating, G. (1985a) *The Production and Use of Forecasts*, London: Methuen.

Keating, G. (1985b) 'The financial sector of the LBS model', London Business School, Centre for Economic Forecasting, mimeo.

Kennedy, P. (1979) *A Guide to Econometrics*, 2nd edn, Oxford: Blackwell.

Laidler, D. E. W. (1982) *Monetarist Perspectives*, Oxford: Philip Allan.

Laidler, D. E. W. and Parkin, J. M. (1975) 'Inflation: a survey', *Economic Journal* 85: 741–809.

Layard, R. (1986) *How to Beat Unemployment*, Oxford: Oxford University Press.

Llewellyn, D. T. (1980) *International Financial Integration*, London: Macmillan.

London Business School (1987) *The LBS model on PC*, London: LBS.

Lucas, R. E. (1976) 'Econometric policy evaluations: a critique', in K. Brunner and A. H. Meltzer (eds) *The Phillips Curve and Labour Markets*, Carnegie Rochester Conferences in Public Policy 1: 19–46, Amsterdam: North Holland.

Lumby, S. (1984) *Investment Appraisal*, 2nd edn, Wokingham: Van Nostrand Reinhold.

McKenna, C. J. (1986) *The Economics of Uncertainty*, Brighton: Wheatsheaf.

McNabb, R. and McKenna, G. (1989) *Inflation in Modern Economies*, Harvester Wheatsheaf.

Meese, R. A. and Rogoff, K. (1983) 'Empirical exchange rate models of the seventies. Do they fit out of sample?', *Journal of International Economics* 14: 3–24.

Morris, E. (ed.) (1985) *The Economic System in the United Kingdom*, 2nd edn, Oxford: Oxford University Press.

Mowl, C. (1980) 'Simulations on the Treasury model', *Government Economic Service Working Pater* 34, London: HM Treasury.

National Institute of Economic and Social Research (1987) *The NIESR Model on PC*, London: NIESR.

Parkin, M. and Bade, R. (1982) *Modern Macroeconomics*, Oxford: Philip Allan.

Pesaran, M. H. and Evans, R. A. (1984) 'Inflation, capital gains and United Kingdom personal savings: 1953: 1981', *Economic Journal* 94: 237–57.

Pindyck, R. S. and Rubinfeld, D. L. (1976) *Econometric Models and Economic Forecasts*, New York: McGraw-Hill.

Pratten, C. (1990) *Applied Macroeconomics*, 2nd edn, Oxford: Oxford University Press.

Richardson, P. (1981) 'Money and prices: a simulation study using the Treasury macroeconomic model', *Government Economics Service Working Paper* 41, London: HM Treasury.

Rostow, W. W. (1978) *The World Economy, History and Prospect*, London: Macmillan.

Shaw, G. K. (1984) *Rational Expectations*, Brighton: Wheatsheaf.

Sheffrin, S. M. (1983) *Rational Expectations*, Cambridge: Cambridge University Press.

Tobin, J. (1981) 'The monetarist counter-revolution, today – an appraisal', *Economic Journal* 91 (361): March.

Treasury, see HM Treasury.

Wallis, K. F., Andrews, M. J., Bell, D. N. F., Fisher, P. G. and Whitley, J. D. (1984) *Models of the United Kingdom Economy*, Oxford: Oxford University Press.

Wallis, K. F., Andrews, M. J., Bell, D. N. F., Fisher, P. G. and Whitley, J. D. (1985) *Models of the United Kingdom Economy: A Second Review*, Oxford: Oxford University Press.

Wallis, K. F., Andrews, M. J., Bell, D. N. F., Fisher, P. G. and Whitley, J. D. (1987) *Models of the United Kingdom Economy: A Fourth Review*, Oxford: Oxford University Press.

Wiener, M. J. (1981) *English Culture and the Decline of the English Spirit*, Cambridge: Cambridge University Press.

Index